Dance With Your Darkness

Shadow Work Guide for Highly Sensitives and Other Powerful Tools to Ease Stress

Ramon Stalenhoef

© **Copyright 2022 - All rights reserved.**

The content contained within this book may not be reproduced, duplicated or transmitted without direct written permission from the author or the publisher.

Under no circumstances will any blame or legal responsibility be held against the publisher, or author, for any damages, reparation, or monetary loss due to the information contained within this book, either directly or indirectly.

Legal Notice:

This book is copyright protected. It is only for personal use. You cannot amend, distribute, sell, use, quote or paraphrase any part, or the content within this book, without the consent of the author or publisher.

Disclaimer Notice:

Please note the information contained within this document is for educational and entertainment purposes only. All effort has been executed to present accurate, up to date, reliable, complete information. No warranties of any kind are declared or implied. Readers acknowledge that the author is not engaged in the rendering of legal, financial, medical or professional advice. The content within this book has been derived from various sources.

Please consult a licensed professional before attempting any techniques outlined in this book.

By reading this document, the reader agrees that under no circumstances is the author responsible for any losses, direct or indirect, that are incurred as a result of the use of the information contained within this document, including, but not limited to, errors, omissions, or inaccuracies.

Table of Contents

INTRODUCTION 1

CHAPTER 1: HIGHLY SENSITIVES AND EMPATHS 7
   WHAT ARE SENSITIVES AND EMPATHS? 10
      Sensitives 10
      Highly Sensitives 11
      Empaths 12
   AM I AN EMPATH, SENSITIVE, OR HIGHLY SENSITIVE? 14
      How Does It Feel to Be an Empath? 15
      How Does It Feel to Be a Sensitive or Highly Sensitive Person? 16
   SCIENCE, MEDITATION, AND SHADOW WORK 17
      The Science of Sensitives 17
      Coping With Being a Sensitive 19
      Sensitives and Shadow Work 20

CHAPTER 2: BRING YOUR SHADOW OUT OF HIDING 23
   BEING GENTLE WITH YOUR SHADOW 23
   WHY YOU NEED TO MEDITATE 27
      Calm Your Overloaded Mind 27
      Bring Your Shadow Self Into the Light 28
   A DANCE WITH YOUR SHADOW 32
      Meditation Transcript 33

CHAPTER 3: THE VULNERABILITY OF HIGHLY SENSITIVES 43
   UNDERSTANDING ENERGY 43
   WHY ARE YOU SO VULNERABLE TO ILLNESS? 47
   YOUR HEALTH IS IMPORTANT TOO 51

CHAPTER 4: THE POWER OF THE PSYCHE 55
   ARE YOU BEING PROGRAMMED? 55
   THE IMPACT OF YOUR MINDSET 60
      Positive 61
      Negative 61
      Growth 61

- Fixed 61
- Optimistic 61
- Pessimistic 62
- Realistic 62
- Unrealistic 62
- FINDING MINDSETS 63
- REPROGRAMMING YOUR MIND 66

CHAPTER 5: FIRST-AID FOR YOUR SOUL 70

- TOOLS TO HEAL YOUR BODY 71
  - Wash Away the Stress 71
  - Use Mudras 71
  - Get Moving 72
  - The Therapy in Smiling 73
  - Eat Well, Be Well 73
  - Crystals—It's Not Magic, It's Science! 74
- HEALING FOR YOUR SOUL 76
  - Breathe In, Breathe Out 76
  - Learn to Detach 78
  - Smoke-Out Your Blues 78
- CAN MY SPIRIT BECOME SICK? 79
  - Purifying Your Aura 79
  - Miraculous Meditation 80
  - Develop an Attitude of Gratitude 81
  - Be Mindfully Kind 82
  - Bells, Chimes, and the Soothing Sound of Water 83

CHAPTER 6: USING SOUND AND SMELL 84

- THE POWER OF MUSIC 84
  - Does Music Have the Ability to Heal? 85
- DIVE INTO DANCING 87
  - Assess Yourself Mentally and Physically 88
  - Pick Your Groove to Move 89
  - This Sensitive's on Fire! 89
  - Slave to the Music 89
  - Go Wild for Five Minutes 90
  - Be Mindful of Your Body 90
  - Do Another Assessment 90
  - Get Ecstatic 91
  - The Story of Petra Biro 91
- ESSENTIAL OILS 92

Soothing Your Soul During Shadow Work *93*

CHAPTER 7: MORE TOOLS TO EASE STRESS 96

HEALING THROUGH NATURE 96
   Nature and Her Desire to Help Us *97*
   Benefits of Forest Bathing *98*
EMOTIONAL FREEDOM TECHNIQUE 100
   How to Practice EFT Tapping *101*
FINDING RELEASE THROUGH MASSAGE THERAPY 102
   How Massage Therapy Improves Shadow Work *103*
HI, I'M YOUR SHADOW; NICE TO MEET YOU 104
   Grounding Yourself—An Essential Embodiment Practice *104*
   Grounded Meditation for Shadow Work *105*
   Why Grounding Is So Powerful *106*
THE BIG FINALE 107
   Dedicate Time and Space *107*
   Shining a Spotlight on Your Shadow *108*
   Accept That Your Shadow Is a Part of You *109*
   Living With All That You Are *110*

CONCLUSION 112

REFERENCES 116

Introduction

I've known Larry for many years. He once told me that as a child, he was bullied mercilessly—the other kids made fun of his sensitivity. Parties were a nightmare to him. While other kids were having a blast, he would soon separate himself from the rest, spending time alone wherever he could find a place to hide. He became overwhelmed with emotions. All the excitement just was too much to bear. Larry didn't understand why he was so different. Even his parents didn't understand. His father tried to use tough love to make him more resilient, but to no avail. It only made Larry feel worse.

Adults liked Larry a lot. He could hold a fluent conversation even when he was only five years old. People said that he had an "old soul," a term used to describe someone wise beyond their years. As Larry grew older, he decided to do research—an effort to discover what was *wrong* with him. But rather than discover that something was wrong, he learned that he was an empath. Still, Larry did not have many friends. Even in high school, he had only one friend.

People were both amazed and afraid because of what he could do. It was as if he could read people's minds. It seemed like he could *talk* to animals and understand them. Some people accused Larry of being a warlock, even some family members! But as this isn't a fantasy novel, that was not the case. His attunement to emotion gave him the ability to tell if someone was hurting, whether mentally or physically. He experienced other people's pain and agony in ways unimaginable—*that's* why he avoided crowds and parties. Although people would be laughing and having a great time, many of them had hurt in their hearts. Larry could feel this, and for some time, didn't understand what he was experiencing.

As an adult, he still doesn't have many friends. Although people like him, they are often too afraid that he may know their secrets. But that's not how being an empath works. An empath often detects intentions, bad emotions, or pain, but is not a mind-reader. As I am a highly sensitive person myself, Larry and I had an instant connection when we met. Considering my experience helping other people in similar situations, I showed Larry how to understand that what he had was not a curse, but a gift. Since I understood full well how difficult it can be to deal with being a sensitive, I have guided many other sensitives to become more accepting of their gifts and how to use them. Today, Larry is using his gift to help others.

In my opinion, there should be more awareness of highly sensitives and empaths. Parents don't always understand what their children are going through, often criticizing their sensitivity instead of celebrating it. My guess is that since you have picked this book, you are a highly sensitive or empath too. What was your childhood like? What is life like for you at the moment? Do you also find it to be a struggle?

The truth is that *all* people have a degree of sensitivity. We must all learn to live with it and embrace it, as it can be of great benefit to us and society. But just as we all have sensitivity, all of us also have a dark side—our "shadow self"—which we try to hide from the rest of the world and ourselves. Some things are just too difficult to deal with, right? We hide this side of ourselves so no one will ever see it, . maybe we even hope that it will just go away. It's just that, hope as we may, it won't. Your shadow self will not just disappear, and nor should it!

This book, *Dance With Your Darkness*, is meant to help you understand your gifts as an empath or highly sensitive person, but more than that, to also understand your shadow self and what part it plays in your life. I will be on this journey with you, guiding you to acceptance and embracing your dark side.

A lonely prisoner will eventually become depressed, making their situation worse. Instead, I will teach you how you can accept this "prisoner," calm them down, find healing, and live a normal and happy life. That is what shadow work is about: turning the oppressed and neglected self into your loyal friend.

Why is it so important to accept your shadow self? First of all, it is a part of you that will not change. When you realize that someone wants to change the person you are, how do you feel? It doesn't feel good, right? In the same way, you have to accept yourself for all there is. Some people may even be shocked at the idea of themselves having a dark side, but it is part of who we all are. It is primal and instinctive, instilled into our being while our ancestors still roamed the Earth, for the main purpose of self-preservation.

Secondly, we all must embrace our dark side as it can interfere with our healing processes if we don't. A lot of hurt, trauma, and painful memories are woven into the fabric of our shadow selves. If we keep pushing it aside, it will never see the light and thereby never be healed. We can try to ignore our shadow selves, but we feel them. They are indeed part of us, so much so, that we can feel the hurt our shadow self is experiencing. If we want complete healing, our complete identity must be revealed. In this way, our joy may be full.

However, this idea in itself is frightening to many people. These people fear that when they allow themselves to experience healing and true joy, something unexpected will happen to rip their joy away. This is in itself a very painful experience. To avoid disappointment, many choose to live without joy. They live in a way that they don't get too happy about things, nor too disappointed or upset. But this way of life is not ideal.

By only looking in front of yourself, not only do you miss out on the majesty of life's mountain tops, but also on the simple beauty of the flowers growing next to the footpath where you're walking. This means that the person does not lead a fulfilling life—if it can be called *life* at all. There is a huge difference between existing and living. To be truly alive, we must be able to take it all in, embracing both the good and the bad as polar opposites, yet an undeniable truth that is in all our being.

To see the light we must first acknowledge that we are in the dark. – Dominic Rouse

For the sake of flow, I will be referring to empaths, sensitives, and highly sensitives only as **sensitives**. For sensitives, inner healing can also be more challenging, as they often criticize themselves easily. While they tend to be kind and forgiving toward others, they can often be harsh toward themselves, expecting nothing but perfection. This is an issue that should be addressed, as all sensitives need to understand it is not in human nature to be perfect. We must embrace our flaws. We must dance with our shadows, carefully planning each step, moving into the flow of our experiences and feelings to make it beautiful.

In this book, you will learn about sensitives, empaths, and highly sensitive people, their similarities and differences, and what this means when it comes to shadow work. Some people (like Larry) do not know that they are sensitives. As I said, we all do have a degree of sensitivity, but for some, the sensitivity weighs more. We will also talk about accepting your shadow self. We will discuss the importance of meditation, where I will provide you with guided meditation, all to give you the opportunity to meet with your shadow self.

We will then examine the link between being a sensitive and being vulnerable to illness. Energy is not some mystic mumbo jumbo, but a scientific reality that influences our lives daily. We will then talk about the importance of your mindset, and how your mind may need reprogramming for the healing to start. We will then take a look at various tips, tricks, and tools you can use for shadow work and complete healing.

If you feel stuck or find that you are judging yourself for lacking the ability to move forward or to heal, this book is for you. You will learn to not only be kind to your side that is always in the sun but your shadow self as well. Your dark side does not need to be something that is feared. It can become an ally, something that can empower you and help you on your journey forward, even helping others along the way.

As a father of two children (a boy, 11, and a girl, 14), I have had my fair share of doubts and fear that some aspects of my shadow self will one day present in them. But that's precisely why I am doing the work now, to understand—and share—how to use my shadow to better myself and the world around me.

I know the anxiety that comes with your shadow self all too well. As I am a highly sensitive person myself, I understand the process of healing and working with the shadow self. I am writing this book for you, as I want to help you become more aware and accepting of both your sensitive nature and your darker side. This will empower you to begin healing yourself, physically, mentally, and spiritually. My hope is that you will be inspired to honor your shadow self, instead of trying to hide it in shame.

I may not know you personally, but still, I want you to become the best version of yourself. Everything you will learn in this book I had to learn myself. It has always been precious to me; a treasure that brought me life in abundance, and I don't want to keep it a secret when it can help other sensitives. I am passionate about your well-being simply because where you are now, I once was. Shadow work and healing did miracles in my life, and I want the same for you.

Perhaps you are not sure whether or not you are a sensitive. If that is the case, don't fret. We'll dive right into it.

Chapter 1:

Highly Sensitives and Empaths

The term **shadow work** can easily create the wrong impression. Some people's minds immediately go to dark and sinister things, such as dark spiritual practices. Some may think that it involves the more malevolent parts within ourselves. This is not the case. Let's talk about what shadow work truly is.

We are all born into dependence. The perspective of the family we are born into will determine what we learn growing up—what we think is acceptable or not. This means that growing up in a broken home can teach a child that dangerous or malicious behavior is acceptable. Everything we are that is viewed as unacceptable by our families is quickly handled and attempts are made at eradicating these traits or behaviors. For the sake of acceptance and survival, we do anything from a young age to suppress these characteristics or behaviors.

Many young people begin to exaggerate behaviors that are approved of to ensure acceptance. Very soon, the aspects that are disapproved of and suppressed are buried in the subconscious mind, while the acceptable behaviors remain in the conscious mind. This may sound like a good idea to some, but it is in fact a person rejecting themselves. That also means that we all have parts of ourselves that we are both aware of and unaware of.

Some liken consciousness to our *light*, as it is something that is open and can easily be observed; while things that are hidden in the subconscious are referred to as our *shadow*. This means that any characteristics, aspects, or behaviors that are not familiar or seen in the light of consciousness, are part of the human shadow, or shadow self. This means that the shadow refers to anything we deny, reject, and perceive as negative. However, our shadow selves do not only contain negative things. There may be many positive things, such as talents, hidden in the shadow.

People who struggle with low self-esteem tend to hide positive aspects of themselves in their shadow self. Let's take Larry, for example. He always thought that there was something wrong with him, only because he was sensitive to other people's emotions. Why? Because his family did not understand it, continually tried to force him to reject that ability. But instead of *fixing* what was wrong with him, it only led to Larry rejecting a part of himself. Today, he understands that experiencing other people's emotions can be a wonderful thing and serve as a beautiful tool to help people in need.

Larry's sensitivity became a part of his shadow. Was this a good thing? I don't think it was. Because of this, he needlessly suffered years of torment and questioning. If only his family did some research to try and understand his gift, rather than try and rip it out of him by using shame and punishment, things would have been a lot different for Larry. Although he is doing better now, years of rejection, misunderstanding, and emotional abuse left their marks. While a person may heal completely, some scars remain.

Other examples may be little boys who are interested in ballet, or playing the piano, perhaps little girls who are interested in guns or cars, but their families say *no*. In itself, there's nothing wrong with talent and interest, but families do determine what is kept in the conscious and the subconscious—the light and the shadow.

How do negative aspects end up in the shadow? Let's say, for example, Pete was a jealous little boy, since he was a toddler. He never liked to share toys or the attention of his parents. When he was a bit older, his parents had a new little boy, Matt. Pete did not like the idea, as the baby now took all of his parents' attention. As Matt turned a bit older, Pete did not want to share toys with him and would use devious schemes to grab his parents' attention away from Matt.

Of course, his parents realized this, regularly punishing Pete for his entitled behavior. They would tell him that it was bad and unacceptable. For fear of losing his parents' love completely (which would not happen easily, though) he chose to bury his own jealousy and force himself to be kinder. Eventually, his role-playing became reality as he became truly kind to his younger brother. What happened with the jealousy? Did it disappear? No, it didn't. It became part of his shadow. The jealous behavior was forced from the conscious to the subconscious.

The problem is that today he may be exerting his jealousy in passive-aggressive ways, perhaps unintentionally hurting those around him. Think about it—instead of just remembering that he was jealous as a child, shouldn't we also wonder *why* he was jealous? Could there have been a reason for it? Perhaps something traumatic happened and it triggered his jealousy. This is why shadow work is important. Even though jealousy in itself can be unnecessary or even ugly, it needs to come to light for healing to start.

Everything we suppress does not simply disappear; it resides in the subconscious. This is the reason we often do things we don't understand. We think to ourselves: *Why did I talk that way? Why was I so rude just now? Why do I feel like crying every night?* These unexplained actions have their roots in our shadow selves.

What Are Sensitives and Empaths?

Sensitive people are divided into three groups: *sensitives*, *highly sensitives*, and *empaths*. Some may view them as being the same, but there are some differences.

Sensitives

Sensitives are more attuned to their senses than non-sensitives. Many people believe that they have a sixth sense, as sensitives are able to detect subtle things others can't. While some sensitives view this as a gift, others find that it creates inner disruption, which can lead to minor or major issues. Minor issues may include becoming distracted or sometimes seeming to be too straightforward. Major issues may include sensitives choosing to avoid crowded places, sometimes confusing others' negative emotions as their own, or having to deal with anxiety. Other sensitives also have to deal with attention deficit hyperactivity disorder (ADHD), some registering on the Autism spectrum. Their biggest difficulty would be being misunderstood.

Growing up as a sensitive is not always easy, especially when their families do not understand why they are acting in certain ways. This causes many sensitives to grow up feeling lonely and often rejected. They love spending time with animals and in nature. People have called sensitives "old souls," as they often have wisdom that is far beyond their years. Sensitives tend to be right-brained people, giving them artistic and creative abilities. They are normally smart and deep thinkers, some being quite philosophical.

If there is a mismatch between their style of learning and the system being used, either in school or at work, they may seem to be unsuccessful or unmotivated. That is only because their brains function differently. A sensitive's brain needs different stimulation and techniques to learn. Even as young children, sensitives often know what is wrong in the world, with things such as institutions and relationships. As they are powerless to change things, it adds to their frustration. Furthermore, they have this full awareness of how things should be, yet as children, they are still too young to truly handle this flood of emotions and thoughts.

They like to talk about things other people or children don't like, which can cause agitation with their peers and some adults. Some may view them as "know-it-alls" and dismiss their thoughts and feelings. This is why sensitives are often alone, even as children.

Highly Sensitives

Highly sensitives share all of the aspects mentioned in the section above. But a *highly sensitive person (HSP)* experiences everything a lot more on the sensitivity scale, such as social, emotional, and physical stimuli. Some people are derogatory against highly sensitives and may accuse them of being melodramatic. In turn, these accusers may seem to be too inconsiderate to a highly sensitive person. Understand that being an HSP does not mean that you have a psychological condition. You simply have heightened responsiveness to both positive and negative influences. It is a rare gift that you should treasure and use for the benefit of society.

An HSP often feels the need to flee from everyone and everything, even if it means spending some time alone in a dark corner, especially after having a hard day or week. It is also easy for them to feel like they are experiencing a sensory overload, such as with clothes that don't fit right, bright lights, or big crowds. They are easily and deeply moved when they see something beautiful, such as in a commercial, movie, nature, art, or another person. Their thoughts and emotions are often rich and complex, which adds to them being misunderstood.

Some highly sensitives struggle to watch violent movies or television shows. They get upset easily when they witness suffering and pain, even if it is make-believe involving either people or animals. An HSP will also often be regarded as being kind and wise, with people always coming to them for advice or comfort.

Highly sensitive people are not so common, making up about 20% of the general population. Unfortunately, many societies choose not to build around highly sensitives, but rather those less sensitive. This is likely to prevent unnecessary issues in the future. Highly sensitive people ask too many questions and like to get things right. Most people choose the easy way of doing things, disregarding deeper thoughts, insights, and wisdom (Scott, 2020).

Empaths

Empaths are right at the top of the sensitivity scale. They are highly tuned into the emotions of people around them, some even experiencing the emotions and physical pain of loved ones miles away. While empaths don't always try to avoid crowds, many people around them can make them feel very uncomfortable. They are often accused of being too sensitive. The life of an empath is like living on a seesaw as they absorb all the feelings of the world—both joys and anxieties.

Doctor Judith Orloff states that empaths lack the filter non-sensitive people have, and as such cannot avoid taking in all of the emotions and pains of people, both loved ones and strangers. According to Kim Egel, a therapist, "empaths have a higher sensitivity to outside stimuli such as sounds, big personalities, and hectic environments. They bring a lot of heart and care to the world and feel things very deeply" (Raypole, 2019).

Empaths can tune in to the emotions or energies of people, places, or animals. Those who are spiritual claim to be sensitive both to things in the seen and the unseen worlds. They are very good at communicating and quickly understand another person's feelings or opinions just by observing their tone, body language, movements, and both the words people use and don't use. They are also quick to realize other people's unspoken perceptions and other energies that may reside within these people.

Larry, as an empath, experienced his sister-in-law's morning sickness *and* cravings before she even knew she was pregnant! He thought that he must have had some kind of stomach ailment, but when he discovered she was pregnant, it all made sense to him. The way he would describe the morning sickness is exactly the same as it would be with a pregnant lady. It has also happened that, while we were talking, he would suddenly say something like *"I have to call my mother."* I would ask *"Why? Did she ask you to?"* He would then reply *"No, but I know she needs me to."* He would then call her, only to find out that either something bad has happened or that she was feeling emotionally down.

We once visited some friends of mine when Larry became unexplainably ill. It was so sudden, we all were shocked. It then turned out that the lady we visited had a son who was ill. Larry had all of his symptoms. I do not know if it is true for all empaths, but many times when Larry was experiencing someone else's pain, morning sickness, or whatever it was, people would say that they started to feel better once Larry shared it with them.

It is as if he is helping them carry the load of their affliction. These are only some examples of his gifts.

Am I an Empath, Sensitive, or Highly Sensitive?

It may be that you can identify with many things we have discussed up to this point, but you may now be wondering: *"Am I a sensitive, HSP, or empath?"*

Let's figure out together to which group you belong. Some people use the terms interchangeably, but in truth, they shouldn't. There is a difference between the three sensitive types. Some think that sensitive people are all meant to have miserable lives for the sake of those around them. This is not accurate at all. Take Larry, for example. Despite all the emotions and feelings he has to endure, he lives a very happy life. Sensitives simply require different things to be happy and fulfilled.

It is possible that you are an HSP and not an empath, or vice versa. The key to understanding the difference lies in the way you experience the world. An HSP experiences stimuli in an amplified manner. This causes an HSP to overthink most things and intensely process all the information they receive. Empaths, on the other hand, are more sensitive to energy. They absorb the energy of people, places, animals, and sometimes objects. An empath is more likely to be spiritual than an HSP.

A similarity between an HSP and an empath is that both can be negatively influenced by their experiences. This is why they need to be trained on how to cope with everything around them to avoid needless suffering.

How Does It Feel to Be an Empath?

People who struggle with emotional baggage or pain see empaths like ships would see a lighthouse. They instantly feel safe in the presence of an empath, even if they are strangers. Empaths often find people approaching them for advice, guidance, or just when they need someone who would listen to them. These can be people known to the empath or someone they just met in a store or at the bus stop. I believe that all people have internal energy. All our energies are constantly reading one another. This is how strangers *know* that they can trust an empath, or just know that this person will listen to them without condemnation or judgment.

Strangers often share their life stories or, surprisingly, secrets—even when the empath is a complete stranger. The empath may not even directly speak with them.

It seems that people use empaths like pitstops to get rid of their heavy load, recharge their souls, and then leave again without thinking about the empaths who helped them. Empaths often know when people are being truthful. They are quick to realize when a person is lying or trying to deceive them or someone else. Sometimes the empath would just have a feeling that something is not right with a person without being able to pinpoint what makes them uncomfortable with the person.

The energy from other people that is absorbed by empaths is similar to a sponge absorbing water—it temporarily becomes part of the empath. Some empaths have difficulty understanding whether they are expressing their own emotions, or projecting the emotions of another person. Places can contain emotions and energies that were left by a person. These energies and emotions can easily be picked up by an empath.

How Does It Feel to Be a Sensitive or Highly Sensitive Person?

Empaths share in all the traits found in an HSP, such as becoming easily overwhelmed by outside stimuli, needing time to be isolated, feeling uncomfortable in crowded places, and being sensitive to smell, sound, and light. It takes longer for all sensitives to destress after a long and demanding day, as it takes some time for their minds and bodies to release all of the stress accumulated during the day. Empaths also have a love for people, animals, and nature, rich and deep thinking, and peaceful environments. While highly sensitives are typically introverts, empaths can be both introverts or extroverts, although the majority of empaths identify as being introverted.

Sensitives or HSPs do not sense energy from others. While they are in tune with others' emotions, they do not absorb these energies. This means that an HSP would experience the emotion of another person without confusing it with their own. Unlike empaths, highly sensitives also do not absorb energy from the places they visit. An HSP isn't necessarily intuitive and spiritual, as it is with empaths.

It can happen, though, that a person can be an HSP *and* an empath. Although it is rare, it does occur. Are you able to place yourself now? Are you a sensitive, highly sensitive, or an empath?

Do you view your abilities as a burden or a blessing? What can you do to help yourself change your perspective, if necessary?

Science, Meditation, and Shadow Work

The reason people resist shadow work is that it deals with aspects that they have suppressed into their subconscious, which are things that are hard to acknowledge. It is admitting that you have a weakness, which some people find too hard to do. You have to directly deal with an aspect of yourself that you have rejected, all for the sake of being accepted and loved. The pain associated with the rejection may surface every time you deal with it through shadow work. Your brain will react by trying to save you from pain—as you feel like you are facing rejection and punishment all over again; as if you are that little kid who had to deal with it before. For shadow work to be a success, you must first accept and love yourself completely for all you are. Honor yourself, both the light and the shadow, while also honoring being a sensitive.

The Science of Sensitives

Sensitives can become easily overwhelmed by their environment. This is because their physical brain is wired differently from those who are not classified as sensitives. According to studies a sensitive's brain displays biological differences from those of others. It appears that perception and experience in people who have higher sensitivity are determined by both their physical sensory processing, as well as emotional processing.

The studies show that those with higher sensory processing sensitivity have biological differences in the Adrenoceptor Alpha 2B (ADRA2B) norepinephrine-related gene variant, the serotonin transporter 5-HTTLPR short or short genotype, and polymorphisms in dopamine neurotransmitter genes. In simpler terms, this means that being a sensitive is not a mental health issue, but something that defines a person, for example, if you have red or brown hair, blue or green eyes, or if you are short or tall. The sensitive cannot help being the way they are and it is not a skill that can be acquired. A study that was published in the Journal of Neuroscience led by Rebecca Todd in 2014, showed that a sensitive's perception of positive and negative images was more vivid than that of other people.

The parts of the brain that are responsible for evaluating whether something is a pleasure or a threat and for regulating emotions were more active with sensitives. This is because the neurotransmitter norepinephrine is influenced by ADRA2B (ScarletScarlet, 2020). As dopamine is your brain's way of rewarding you when you have behaved in a certain way or did something your brain wants you to repeat, your brain will likely secrete more dopamine when you do things differently, such as spending time alone. In this way, your brain is using dopamine to protect you, rewarding you for avoiding situations that could be overwhelming. As such, sensitives are not drawn to external rewards like other people are.

"Mirror neurons" are used to determine the motive or mood of another person or to predict their actions. While you are observing another person, your mirror neurons are used to compare the person's behavior to when your own behavior was similar. In this way, your mirror neurons are trying to uncover why this person is acting in a certain way by mentally placing you in that person's shoes. While all people have mirror neurons, they are more active in the brains of sensitives. This is why it is so easy for a sensitive to pick up whether someone has good or bad intentions.

The parts of the brain that process sensory data and regulate emotions and values are all connected to the ventromedial prefrontal cortex (vmPFC). In sensitives, this part of the brain is more active, which means that sensitives experience emotions more intensely. It is not about a more intense outside experience in this regard but has to do with more vivid processing of emotions within the mind of the sensitive.

Coping With Being a Sensitive

Due to becoming easily overwhelmed, many find that being sensitive is rather challenging.

How can you cope with being a sensitive? Think about all that makes being a sensitive a gift instead of a burden. Decide to be grateful for your abilities and to honor and respect yourself for being such a wonderfully unique and rare individual.

Sensitives seem to mostly know how to use their words, and when to use them. They often carefully consider when to engage in a conversation and when to avoid it. Sensitives care deeply about others, many viewing themselves as healers. Many sensitives find it easy to solve problems as they can piece things together to view them as a whole. Most sensitives are creative, with careers or interests in music, telling stories, writing, and acting.

Sensitives are often visionaries, carefully determining the consequences of their actions, and whether they would be beneficial to society and the planet in the long run. Because sensitives love to analyze and inspect everything from every corner, they are able to make great decisions, which makes them efficient leaders. Sensitives often come to deep realizations and wisdom that they love to share with others, enriching the lives of those around them. How often do you feel urged to share newfound wisdom and insights with others? How do you feel when you witness your insight improving the lives of others?

Sensitives and Shadow Work

Because you have suppressed rejected aspects of yourself into your shadow self, you will feel that these aspects only cause embarrassment and are worthy of rejection. This is why you would not want these aspects to surface. However, when certain things happen in our lives, aspects in our shadow may trigger unwanted behaviors and emotions. For this reason, shadow work requires full self-acceptance, self-love, courage, guidance, and self-awareness to face your shadow self and deal with it in a healthy manner. We can never get rid of any part of our character, only suppress it, making shadow work the way to integrate everything that defines us, carefully, without feeling anxious or rejected.

Shadow work can help you become your authentic self, with no part of you being rejected or suppressed. Doing shadow work also requires patience and determination, as rushing it will only lead to frustration. Doing shadow work is exhausting; still, you want to minimize exhaustion and not add any unnecessary stress while doing it. Ensure that you are willing to love and accept yourself completely, both the light and the shadow. You can do shadow work on your own, but you should consult with a qualified therapist if you have to deal with severe trauma.

Again, your shadow is not a mistake that was made or a flaw in your character. If there are traits that you don't want to include in the visible part of your identity, shadow work can help you control them. Other aspects that are socially acceptable can be integrated into your personality and identity. With the help of shadow work, you don't need to feel ashamed of these characteristics, but rather honor and embrace them. This will greatly improve your self-esteem and boost your confidence, as you won't need to live with the fear that this unknown part of yourself will eventually come into the light.

Many people hide their artistic side in the shadow because of ridicule and shame, often by loved ones and family members. Through shadow work, you can accept your artistic side, learn to love it, and then begin to use it in your creative expressions. Boys are sometimes denied their want to play the piano or become painters, while girls may be discouraged to express themselves through certain music genres, such as rap. There may be a beautiful and artistic side to yourself that has been suppressed for too long. It is time to bring it to the surface.

When we have certain traits that are rejected, we may project negative emotions, thoughts, and feelings toward others when we recognize similar traits. Therefore, when you do shadow work, your relationships will also improve with family members, friends, colleagues, and others who cross your path. Shadow work will also teach you to have true compassion for yourself, alleviating negative self-talk and self-judgment. You will also experience more compassion toward others as you overcome your hidden issues.

Your overall well-being will improve, physically and mentally, as you release anxiety and overcome false beliefs. We often act or think in ways that can be hurtful toward ourselves or others. Through shadow work, you'll have a better understanding of why you are behaving in certain ways or what shapes your thoughts.

As we have seen, the brain of a sensitive is wired differently. Therefore, sensitives need to take a different approach to shadow work. You have feelings and boundaries and for this reason, you must put your own mind and body first. Never push yourself too fast or too far when doing shadow work. Be gentle with yourself and have tons of patience. You may get stuck. If that happens, don't judge yourself. Some sensitives give up on shadow work because they burn themselves out, trying to rush results. Choose to honor your shadow, rather than try to remove or destroy it.

Don't try shadow work if you are not ready to accept and love yourself fully. First, decide that you will build on your self-esteem. Doing shadow work with low self-esteem can do more damage than good. Understand that you will face things that you do not like, things that you want to reject and discard. You will have to accept all of it as part of who you are. This is why you need to love yourself completely. It is time that you embrace yourself, both the light and the dark.

Through this book, I will take you by the hand and provide you with all the tools you need to make shadow work a healing success. We won't rush, judge, or criticize, but look at ourselves with love, compassion, and hope, honoring the gift of our sensitive nature.

Chapter 2:

Bring Your Shadow out of Hiding

Too many people today are drowning in stress and anxiety. A lot of this can be ascribed to their subconscious, often bringing forth unwanted behaviors. Every person needs to do shadow work. It will help confront fears and anxieties, help the person embrace both their light and shadow, and bring healing where it is necessary. For shadow work to be successful, you need to bring your shadow self into the light. Sensitives, however, need to take their sensitive nature into account. Shadow work cannot be rushed or pushed, especially in the case of sensitives. The sensitive must approach shadow work carefully to avoid any harm or overwhelming feelings of resistance. This is where meditation comes in—it helps the sensitive to gently, calmly, and kindly allow their shadow to surface for mental and physical healing to begin.

Being Gentle With Your Shadow

True self-love means to accept all of who you are, including what is suppressed into your shadow self. Learning this kind of love can be challenging, especially if you are regularly in an environment filled with toxic people or an environment that is overall depressing. We often get labeled by others, which can also make loving ourselves harder. You may also be struggling with constant negative thoughts brought on by past trauma or judgments. What if you grew up with no positive role models? Some people can't love themselves simply because of what they see in the mirror. This is often caused by bullying, ridicule, and body shaming.

We should all celebrate who we are. Life is filled with ups and downs, from moments when we think we're the best to moments when we couldn't hate ourselves more. Society makes a great effort in teaching everyone to be mindful of others, which is a good thing, but we should also be mindful of ourselves. When the time comes when you would normally berate and loathe yourself, be mindful of who you are. Understand that everyone goes through cycles of success and failure. Make mindfulness your foundation of love. Then, when bad times come, you won't resort to self-loathing, but rather to self-compassion.

Attaining a healthy love for yourself is not being selfish. Some live by the notion that you don't need to love yourself to give love, but that is not true. How can you give someone water from an empty cup? It needs to be filled with water first before you can share it with others. Love is the same. You need to fill yourself with love, then, the love you share with others will be pure, unconditional, and unbreakable.

Many things that were suppressed into our shadow were caused by things we were told in our childhood, however, as adults we still have to endure criticism and sometimes ungrounded opinions of others. It is therefore important to identify which words help promote our character and which are detrimental.

You have the fullest right to say *"No, I won't make those words my own. I won't take them to heart."* Some may even become upset when you resist their opinion, but when you have identified their words as negative and non-constructive, you must protect yourself by refusing to entertain these opinions. Identify the bullies who often pretend to have your best interest at heart, but are cunning in finding ways to try and bring you down, or shove your character into a box.

On the other hand, we all have flaws. Sometimes a good friend will point out mistakes we make, trying to teach us not to repeat bad behavior, or stop us from making the wrong choices. As we are pressured to do, we believe that we should be perfect. Therefore, any mistake being pointed out feels like an attack on our personalities. Here too, we should discern the intention of the person sharing their opinion or guidance. If what they say is true, feel the sting but don't get angry. Rather embrace the fact that we all have flaws, and see this intervention as an opportunity to learn, grow, and become a better version of yourself.

How do you treat your best friend? Do you belittle them whenever they make a mistake? Do you shower them with negative words when they want to try something new or need some wisdom or encouragement? Most likely you don't, right? When someone is your best friend, you'll be kind and compassionate toward them. You will try and make their world a better place, making sure that they know you are there for them, willing to hold their hand when they need you to. Why can't we be the same person toward ourselves? We are in our own company every second of every day. Befriend yourself. Instead of saying harsh things to yourself, imagine that you are talking to your best friend. Treat yourself the same you would treat your friend. Be kind and supportive toward yourself.

What you do to or for yourself influences your subconscious mind. If you are constantly judging and criticizing yourself unnecessarily, your subconscious will accept that you are *not worth it*. That is dangerous! This is why you must learn to care for yourself. Start small, such as taking a longer bath, treating yourself to a massage, or cooking a healthy and nutritious meal. Even small acts of kindness and self-care will have a positive impact on your subconscious, proving (to yourself) that you are worthy of love and care. It may be difficult at first, especially if

25

you believe that you are not entitled to self-care. Make a conscious decision, and every time you want to punish or criticize yourself, choose to turn it around. Choose that you *will* care for and love yourself.

One of the best things you can do to promote self-love is shadow work. As you know by now, shadow work is intense and can be painful. While shadow work entails bringing hidden characteristics and aspects to light, embracing and accepting them as part of who you are, some shadow work is about excavating and changing your core beliefs. Some parts of our shadow *can* be changed. Examples of core beliefs hidden in your shadow may be: *I'll never be good enough, I'm not smart, No one likes me, I shouldn't be among people.* Many core beliefs are false and should be identified as such. Then, you can begin working on changing these beliefs into something constructive and positive.

Sensitives often act as advocates for others and are not afraid to stand up for them when an injustice is being done. What about you? Do you always stand up for the rights of others? But what about yourself? Unfortunately, sensitives are often critical and impatient with themselves, not willing to tolerate the smallest of mistakes they make.

Instead, choose to be your own advocate. Learn to stand up for yourself, whether you are attacked by another person or if you are struggling with negative self-talk. Choose a kinder and more constructive approach. Do this by acknowledging and honoring your needs, feelings, and values, regardless if it means that you have to protect yourself from yourself.

Why You Need to Meditate

Meditation is an effective way to induce relaxation, both physically and mentally. This is why it is the ideal way to allow your shadow self to surface. Meditation is not new—it has been practiced for millennia, today becoming a rapidly growing trend in the U.S. and other parts of the world. Anyone can practice meditation. There are no limitations as to who can practice it regarding religion, income, status, or culture. Let's talk about the benefits of meditation.

Calm Your Overloaded Mind

Many sensitives find that meditation is ideal for calming down their busy and overloaded minds. There are some misconceptions about meditation, such as you *have* to open your third eye, or your mind must be cleared of all thoughts. This is not altogether true. An effective session may include simply sitting in a tranquil environment, closing your eyes, and focusing on your breathing. When thoughts come, and they probably will, acknowledge the thoughts and let them pass by, instead of trying to silence them or shove them away.

Finding a meditation type and technique that will work for you may take some time and effort. An effective method of meditation is just as unique as the meditator themselves. Although meditation can be used as a spiritual practice, as it has been done since ancient times, we don't need to use meditation as a spiritual tool. We can also use meditation for improving our mental and physical well-being. There are countless different types and methods of meditation, and you will have to find the method that works for you. I will make it easier than having to find your own method first, saving you a lot of time. I've designed a unique meditation for you that you will find in the last sub-section of this chapter, *A Dance With Your Shadow*.

Breathing meditation uses the technique of focusing on your breathing, while object meditation focuses on an object, such as a candle, a smell such as incense, a sound such as a gong, or a feeling such as sitting in a breeze. Movement meditation includes walking or dancing while being focused on your movements and feelings in your body, your arms, legs, and every move you make. There are so many choices and combinations—find what works for you and meditate daily. It will train your mind and enhance your ability to process environmental stimuli during your day.

Bring Your Shadow Self Into the Light

Many people report that they have discovered things about themselves while meditating. Some of these things are great, while others are not as pleasant. The aspects they discover that are not pleasant are things that have surfaced from the shadow. This means that many meditators, unbeknownst to themselves, have already started with shadow work. Meeting your shadow self will likely be painful, but is a crucial part of finding complete healing.

Things that come to light during meditation may include:
- complexes, which are things you may be fixated on, such as the success of a sibling
- fears that are hidden in your subconscious, such as a numbing fear of losing everything
- traumas that have been suppressed
- shameful feelings such as guilt or regret
- negative thoughts such as telling yourself that you are not good enough or worthy of love
- unresolved and difficult emotional issues, such as anger and aggressiveness
- wild desires, which can cause a person to question their sexual identity
- Many good things can also surface, but to the person would seem necessary to suppress, such as:
    - hidden talents
    - deep compassion (especially when it is a sensitive male, families may frown upon their sensitivity and compassion)
    - suppressed cognitive abilities, such as being able to become a grade-A student, but never having the opportunity to do so
    - rejected gender identity

Sensitives who are new to meditating often complain that it makes them feel worse, as if their minds are becoming more busy or noisy. This is a misconception on their part. As meditation brings suppressed aspects to the surface, their minds are more aware of things that are already there. It is like peeling fruit to find a worm inside—peeling the fruit did not place the worm there, it was there to begin with. This means that, before you start meditating, decide that you are willing to bring your shadow into the light. Decide on your intention—that you are going to liberate your shadow self, allowing it to receive the love and honor it deserves. It is part of you after all.

According to a study published in the *Journal of Cognitive Psychotherapy* (Coholic, 2005), participants in the study reported a significant spiritual experience while meditating. They reported higher levels of self-awareness, felt more compassion toward aspects of their shadow, felt whole and integrated as a complete person, experienced a calm mind, and an increase in their self-esteem, self-respect, and self-confidence. This shows that meditation has a highly positive impact on the life of the meditator.

Let's discuss some meditation techniques you can use.

Meditation for Relaxation

This type of meditation is focused on relaxing both your body and your mind. You may be prompted to use breathing as a technique, for example: *Take four deep breaths, breathe in through your nose, exhale through your mouth.*

To make these sessions more efficient, try and learn the process, so you can do it without listening to a prompt. This will help your brain to relax and destress even more.

Focused Attention Meditation

This technique is used to train your brain's ability to focus. During the session, you have to focus on something specific, such as your breathing, counting your breaths, looking at a candle, or listening to the sound of a fountain or wind chime. The goal is for your mind to become as quiet as possible. Those who have mastered this technique have little difficulty concentrating, for example, when they are working in a noisy environment, the noises do not distract them easily.

Mindfulness Meditation

The goal of this method is to completely calm your mind. You will be aware of your thoughts and acknowledge them, however, you won't react to them emotionally or physically. Every thought is looked at objectively. With this kind of calmness, you'll easily be able to see which thoughts are constructive and which are harmful. However, you do not judge any of your thoughts while examining them.

Transcendental Meditation and Christian Centering Prayer

The meditator uses a mantra or a Christian prayer to focus on. Whenever their thoughts are wandering, the meditator brings the thoughts back in a calm manner, by returning their focus to the mantra or prayer. The meditator repeats this technique until the *noise* of the mind has disappeared. This means that the meditator who has mastered it will experience a tranquil mind throughout the day, even while not meditating.

Simple Guided Meditation

You have the choice of doing guided meditation either with a professional, while reading a book, or listening to a recorded voice. The meditation will have you imagine being on a path or a journey while imagining that someone is with you to serve as a guide. It can help you visualize reaching goals or breaking bad habits. However, with this type of meditation, your brain is still active, even though your body is feeling relaxed. The intent of this method is for preparing your mind and empowering it to reach goals and for other achievements, and can be used to discover more about your shadow self.

A Dance With Your Shadow

In this section, you will find a guided meditation especially crafted for sensitives. It aims to honor your sensitive nature and find healing. My intent with this technique is to help you find your shadow, make peace with it, and embrace it as part of yourself.

If you are reading this in print, take a moment to stretch, then find yourself a piece of technology with which you are comfortable. This exercise should take just over twenty minutes as that is the duration of the soothing recording of this guided meditation, which can be found here: tinyurl.com/tomeditation

I have provided the meditation script if you would like to prepare yourself for what's coming or if you would like to read it after listening to it:

Meditation Transcript

Please make yourself comfortable lying down on your bed, seated, or wherever you can be completely comfortable.

Allow your eyes to close and take a few moments to scan your awareness through the sensations of your body.

Allow your attention to gently come into the body to the flowing of your breath.

Experience the sense of your body as a whole, simply lying here, extended, and breathing.

The more you allow yourself to connect to your innate sensitive gifts, the more you can heal yourself.

When you feel ready, picture in your mind's eye the image of a large and beautifully decorated ballroom. You're standing in the middle of the room and you notice some beautiful details.

Just see if you can bring that image into vivid focus in your mind's eye.

Take another deep breath and ground yourself.

Notice how this place slows you down.

Look down and feel the ground under your feet.

As you watch the floor carefully, you'll notice that it can change colors.

And they move.

Vibrant colors paint the floor like northern lights dancing through the sky.

Wow, this floor is like a palette of flying colors. It looks bright and playful.

Wait, you notice you can influence the colors.

And the shapes. And the movements.

You are in control of the floor. In some kind of way, your consciousness is connected to this floor.

Now, just imagine the floor turning into the most beautiful purple colors.

You see? You just turned it into purple.

Now ask the colors to move and to change shape.

Wow, you just created a floor full of flying colors.

Just look at it, and play with it for a moment.

It's connected to you. Actually, it feels part of you.

This ballroom is a wonderful place where your thoughts become real.

Standing here, being here in this place gives you new possibilities to change your reality.

It feels powerful to have control over this floor with your conscious mind.

Here you can tap into your innate manifesting powers that are always available to you.

You can change reality with each thought... and with each breath.

See what happens when you fully inhale... expanding your belly and chest as much as you can.

Holding it for a moment...

And exhale...

Notice what you do to the floor when you breathe in and out...

Inhale... filling your entire breathing system with fresh oxygen.

Hold it...

And exhale...

Inhale... so that you are brimming with air.

Holding it... soaking in oxygen...

And exhale... your body relaxes, without any effort...

Fully inhale... feeling these fresh breaths purifying your entire body...

Exhale... Take note of how you feel at this very moment and how you influence the floor with your calm state of mind.

You now have an abundance of oxygen.

This is what makes you feel alive, how we are created to feel.

Let the flow of your breath become natural and notice how strong you feel.

Good.

Now visualize yourself standing on the floor of the ballroom again. No one else is around... Everything is calm and peaceful...

Just look around, noticing the beauty all around you... you are fully relaxed.

Now take a look at the floor. You feel safe and grounded. You are looking at it from a place of love. I would like to invite you to make it pitch-black.

Just ask… Great, you already did.

This darkness is part of who you are. You are made of both dark and light aspects.

And within your darkness lies some of the most worthwhile inner work you can do as a human being.

Prepare to meet some aspect of yourself you'd rather not think about. We all have tucked things away in our own shadow. Our own darkness.

Feeling grounded and strong in this ballroom of empowerment, you're now connected with it.

To meet your shadow in a safe way, I will help you… to dance with your darkness.

Prepare yourself for healing. You will look the dark aspect of yourself in its eyes and face it fully. To release it fully. Dance step-by-dance step.

Please repeat after me, to get fully prepared:

"I am safe."

"I am strong."

"My sensitivity is my superpower."

"I am stronger than I think."

"I can let go of the past to embrace my future."

You notice that the floor is completely dark. Actually, the whole ballroom is dark now. You can hardly see anything.

This darkness is a change to invite and shine your inner light… and to get a clear view of the aspects of your shadow self that you've been hiding in the dark.

Accept it and integrate it. I will guide you.

As you just become increasingly comfortable in following the natural rhythm of the breath, I'd just like you to imagine now a steady flow of light from the top of your head.

It flows almost like liquid sunlight.

It's very smooth, very warm, very clear, very bright.

This is your inner light.

It flows down through the top of the head, into the body, and travels all the way down.

Just melting away any tension, any discomfort. In this quiet and peaceful state, your inner light chased away any limiting beliefs. You feel safe, strong, and confident.

Even though the entire body now is full of that very spacious, clear feeling, it continues to flow outward.

You notice your inner light, which illuminates the space around you. Like you're standing in an aura of light.

This is the moment to shine your inner light onto your shadow. Invite your shadow to appear in the light. Just ask if it can come out of the darkness of the floor and see what's manifesting.

Watch it slowly becoming visible. Rising from the dark.

Your shadow is illuminated by your inner light now.

Don't question what you see. This is the aspect of yourself that you put away, that has been hurt, traumatized, or repressed.

Even if nothing visual appears, that's alright. Your shadow may also show itself as a feeling, strong or subtle. Give it time. Let your shadow fully manifest.

Feel its anger, its sadness, or whatever else comes up. Maybe a painful memory or an unhealthy belief. It's all fine. Having feelings is not a weakness. Being sensitive is your greatest strength. You are sensitive and strong.

You've become aware of your shadow… It's right in front of you.

Just touch it. Carefully. And make peace with it.

Welcome it.

Accept it.

Forgive it.

Embrace it.

Hold it close and slowly start your dance.

Do the moves that feel best for you. You may gradually increase the size of your movement. You don't have to think about your steps. You're just dancing.

It balances your shadow and your light and you will appreciate yourself on a new and deeper level. Love your shadow for all it is. Give it your love and compassion. Without judgment.

This dance is essentially emotion in motion.

How does it feel to dance with your darkness? Allow feelings of love and compassion to move through your body.

Hold your shadow close to your heart and feel the connection.

This is the moment you created the loving space to ask some questions to your shadow. Just keep on dancing and take some time to let the answers flow.

Ask your shadow, "What can I give you? What will help you?"

Take some time to let the answers flow. Allow for yourself to experience any insightful messages.

"What do you want from me?"

"How can you help me?"

"Which lesson do you want to teach me?"

Thank your shadow. Feel thankful for the opportunity to connect.

By embracing your shadow, you become whole.

Remember, your light cannot exist without your darkness. Your enlightened side cannot exist without the darker aspect of your personality.

This dance creates harmony within, and aligns you to your spiritual core.

Connecting with your shadow is an act of self-love. Your loving awareness is so powerful.

Now, while you're still dancing and holding your darkness in your heart space, shine your inner light brighter and brighter and notice, when you do this, your shadow fades away more and more.

It's not disappearing. It's merging. Your inner light embraces your inner darkness.

Healing is happening. This dance is a process of becoming whole again.

Think about it... How can you completely and wholeheartedly accept who you are if there are sides of yourself that you're too afraid to explore?

If you stop dancing now and look at the floor, you notice, that the darkness is still dancing in the light. They have found each other. Like yin and yang.

Now, take your time to bring back your attention to your body again.

Whenever you are ready, take another nice deep breath and become fully aware of the present moment, ready to take on the rest of your day with confidence.

Faith is the light that guides you through the darkness.

Take heart and decide to be unashamedly yourself… Move on and stay strong.

Chapter 3:

The Vulnerability of Highly Sensitives

This may be difficult but good to know, further validating why shadow work is so important. Sensitives are more prone to illness than non-sensitives, as suppressed negative emotions are more challenging for sensitives to deal with, and they are also easily overstimulated. A sensitive's shadow self can make them ill. With this being said, the opposite is true as well—positive emotions and mindsets promote physical wellness. Especially with sensitives, it is a question of mind over matter when it comes to health.

Understanding Energy

Everything in your environment has a frequency or energetic vibration. Sensitives are tuned into these frequencies, even noticing small changes. Sensitives sometimes absorb foreign energies which then become part of their bodies. For this reason, sensitives must train how to block foreign and especially unwanted energies, avoiding these from affecting them. Words that are thought, read, or spoken have a distinct energy pattern, depending on the intention of the person who is the source of the words. An emotional response follows which is determined by the energy pattern.

Did you know that a word that is spoken becomes empowered and fueled with energy? Let's take the word "detest" for example. This word can immediately cause an emotional response, whether it is spoken, read, or thought. The source of the word adds its own energy as well: Supposing the person did not speak the word but only thought it, the word would still resonate with enough energy to be picked up by a sensitive, even if the person's body language or facial expression couldn't be used as visible clues. This adds some light to the origins of the phrase "getting a vibe."

We find reports of mind over matter throughout many cultures. According to the Merriam-Webster dictionary, the concept of *mind over matter* is defined as "a situation in which someone is able to control a physical condition, problem, etc., by using the mind." The idea of mind over matter seems far fetched, but is it possible that it is rooted in some reality?

According to the Institute of Noetic Sciences (2016), scientists interested in this phenomenon have been conducting experiments for almost a century. Doctor Joseph Banks Rhine conducted such experiments in the 1930s, though those were basic when compared to today's standards. The tests aimed to determine whether people have the ability to manipulate an outcome, such as dice being thrown. Surprisingly, these experiments yielded positive results.

The first *random number generator (RNG)*, was invented by a physicist, Doctor Helmut Schmidt, in the 1970s. The machine worked as electrons were released from a small piece of lightly radioactive material. Participants in the study would be asked to think of numbers while looking at the machine. Again, to everyone's amazement, the results showed that the machine's generated numbers leaned more toward the intended choices of the participants, deviating from its baseline. This means that the participants' intentions influenced the machine. Although the effect wasn't enormous, the results were still significant.

Years later, Doctors Robert Jahn and Brenda Dunne confirmed these results through experiments that were done at the Princeton Engineering Anomalies Research Laboratory (PEAR). When participants were asked to concentrate on higher or lower numbers, the output again deviated from randomness to match their intent. Research conducted at the Institute of Noetic Sciences finds that shared emotions and mental states also influence the RNGs. Princeton's scientist and psychologist, Roger D. Nelson, is in charge of research being done on a global scale—The Global Consciousness Project. His idea (which was executed) was to place RNGs worldwide among populations. Nelson predicted that the RNGs will be influenced by people as their attention was captured by global events. Over the course of 20 years, over 500 significant worldwide events triggered the RNGs, again causing them to deviate from randomness. Events included natural disasters, terrorist attacks, and New Year celebrations. The odds that this would only happen by chance is more than a trillion to one.

Although scientists are able to prove that the intention of people influences the RNGs, how it happens is still a mystery and something they cannot explain. Their findings, though, show that order appears from the intention of the masses. This also proves that people's consciousness has an influence on the physical world. It also means that the mind plays an important part in perceived reality.

Doctor Bruce Lipton, who is a molecular biologist, author, stem cell specialist, and winner of the 2009 Goi Peace Award, has an understanding of the energies that surround us and are within us, and he specifically studies vibrations and thoughts. Doctor Lipton's studies at the Stanford Medical School focused on mind over matter and proved scientifically how the mind, body, and spirit are connected. Doctor Lipton aimed to prove that our thoughts influence our bodies (Glad.is Admin, 2020).

According to Doctor Lipton, communication starts with energy and vibrations. While there is a large number of different types of energy, vibrations can basically be divided into two categories—good and bad vibrations. Bad vibrations drain your energy, while good vibrations give you more energy. Our bodies do not interpret vibrations into words or logical thoughts. We only feel whether vibrations are good or bad.

Have you ever experienced someone who tends to drain your energy? Some people can leave you feeling fatigued only after spending a short while with them, with no activities but talking. You may know other people, on the other hand, who leave you feeling more motivated and energetic than before. Have you ever met a person who just gave you "bad vibes"? I'm not talking about judging a person, but about that inward feeling you get. This happens especially when you are a sensitive.

In my personal experience, I have met people who gave me such bad vibes, only to find out later that there was a good reason for me feeling that way. One such instance was when I met a friend of a family member. I even warned my family member about this person, picking up on this *friend's* bad intentions. It turned out afterward that the person stole from my friend and eventually ended up in jail.

Animals can read energy and vibrations as well. Similar to humans, some animals are highly sensitive too. They are necessary for the survival of their species. We have all heard about cases where dogs do not trust certain people. More often than not it is for a good reason. Dogs aren't mind readers, but animals pick up on energies and are able to distinguish good from bad vibrations. Such is the case when animals flee from an area before a natural disaster strikes. It's all about the vibrations they read from the environment. Life is based on energy—when something has energy, it is alive, when there is no energy, there is no life. Perhaps this is why many spiritual practices believe that everything, including every rock, plant, and animal has life. What causes vibrations to be either bad or good?

It is based on what you believe. The things we believe determine how we think and what our attitudes will be. When you constantly have bad thoughts and emotions, do you think your vibrations will be good? This means that to change your vibrations, you need to change any false beliefs you may have and correct your mindset from negative to positive, thereby changing your perspective and attitude toward life.

Why Are You So Vulnerable to Illness?

Research done on over 100 different animal species has shown that 15–30% of all populations are highly sensitive to their environments. This is true for people as well, affecting over 1 billion people worldwide (Rosieraleigh, 2019). Making an effort to understand their sensitivity will make the world a better place, whether you are highly sensitive or non-sensitive. Sensitives often feel isolated because of their differences compared to non-sensitives, and non-sensitives are sometimes too quick to judge, as they don't know what being sensitive is about.

One in five people are sensitives, often struggling with illnesses more intensely than non-sensitives. Their feelings of isolation do not help, making them feel worse, and preventing them from reaching their goals and living their dreams. Sensitives are more prone to illness as they easily become overstimulated by their environment and circumstances. Ill health has a negative influence on the economy, as sensitives who are ill cannot continually carry the workload they are supposed to. This harms their careers and can lead to burnout. Some sensitives leave the workforce altogether because of its negative impact on their health.

Because sensitives often feel isolated, some of them marginalize themselves, which prevents them from sharing their talents and innovations with the workforce or the rest of the community. Instead of embracing cognitive diversity (as it realistically exists in the world), many companies focus on creating something called *groupthink*, where it is assumed that all employees will have the same cognitive processes, in other words, think exactly the same. But is this viable? Sensitives are more in tune with other people and their environment, and with their deep thinking, are often more creative.

By embracing cognitive diversity instead of relying on running a company with a *hive mind*, these companies will find it beneficial in terms of greater workflow and innovativeness. In turn, this will have a very positive impact on the economy. Learning how to understand sensitives may help companies put preventative measures in place to avoid the overstimulation and burnout of their sensitive employees. In the study mentioned earlier in this section, scientists have also found that the sensitive part of animal populations ensures their survival. This 15–30% of the highly sensitive animals are more tuned in to their environment, therefore are able to know early on when danger is coming.

This is also true with humans, where companies can benefit from their sensitivity. Sensitives will be able to pick up quickly if something is wrong or when the company is in danger. But for this to work, companies will have to accept that part of their workforce falls under those who are sensitive, highly sensitive, or empathic. In the same way, sensitives will also benefit from a positive environment, which means the company should take better care to ensure the well-being of all their employees, acknowledging and listening to the needs of working for them.

Society has a number of norms that everyone is sup by. Sensitives understand this and force themselves ..ve up to this norm, whether they can handle it or not. This is what causes illness in sensitives involved in the workforce. Unfortunately, instead of reaping the benefits of having sensitives in their employ, companies miss the opportunity to have someone who can spot danger from afar, saving their employers time and money. Sensitive employees end up being marginalized and in ill health as their needs are neglected.

Besides work-related stresses and obligations, several other things in life can be emotionally demanding. Such things can include having to work on maintaining healthy relationships, feeling the pressure of having to succeed, having a fear that you'll miss out on things, and being expected to keep up with everything new. Unfortunately, most people have become adept at hiding their emotions. Why? Because people are often encouraged to push their emotions aside. Some believe that by ignoring emotions, they will simply *go away*. But this can't be further from the truth.

How do people attempt to bury their emotions? They do it through the use of technology, spending excessive time on social media or watching television, some turn to drugs or alcohol, or both, to suppress certain emotions, and some abuse prescribed medication. A time may come when a person *has* to face and acknowledge their emotions, but they are quickly dismissed by using phrases such as *"Get over it, it's life,"* or *"Don't let it bother you."* These phrases may sound like good advice, but it only ends up in the emotions being bottled, which is detrimental to both your physical and mental health.

Imagine you are visiting Wyoming, and decide to go to Yellowstone National Park. You are excited to see Old Faithful.

...er waiting for about 40 minutes, the geyser erupts, spewing water almost 100 feet into the air. What causes this? Magma that is present two to five miles under the surface heats the water, creating pressure. Soon, the water can't be contained, and it erupts. I'm sure you have heard that someone has "exploded" with anger. Maybe it happened to you.

People are surprised when this happens, but they shouldn't be. Why does it happen that a person suddenly explodes? It happens because of emotions that are ignored. Just like the water of Old Faithful, suppressed emotions build up inside of you. When the pressure becomes too much, you erupt with anger. Emotions that are dealt with do not have a chance to create pressure; they have energy which means they need to be expressed. Our bodies, thinking they were smart, learned how to suppress them. We still hold our breaths and contract our muscles to suppress our emotions.

Emotions that are ignored, however, do not only put you in danger of exploding, but also can cause anxiety and depression. When your brain decides that emotions are too conflicting or overwhelming, it decides to thwart these emotions. This causes a great deal of stress on both your body and mind. Such emotional stress can cause mental health issues and also physical ailments, such as headaches, autoimmune disorders, heart disease, insomnia, and intestinal problems. Mind over matter, remember? This is its power—not only can your mind influence what happens in your environment, but also in your body.

Bottled emotions can also cause you to lash out at people, even if they don't really deserve it. It's easy to get caught up in heightened emotions when other worse emotions are not dealt with. Someone may ask you an innocent question but because of buried emotions, it triggers anxiety or anger within you. As emotions have energy they need to flow freely and without constraint. It is unfortunate that society expects us to hide our emotions, especially when it comes to males. *"Boys don't cry"* or

"You're a big girl now"—do these sound familiar? We are taught to bottle emotions even at a very young age.

The irony is that we bottle our emotions for fear of facing them, refusing to give emotions some kind of control over us. Yet, if we ignore our emotions, they end up controlling us. We experience uncontrollable outbursts or fits of rage because of triggers caused by unresolved issues associated with emotions. It can cause us to become rude or mean, distrustful, and overall negative. This can't lead to a happy life. Isn't it time to take control and consciously decide to become happy? I think it is. Especially if you are a sensitive.

When emotions are triggered in the midbrain, the vagus nerve responds by sending signals to the intestines, lungs, and heart. This causes a state of anxiety as the brain attempts to warn the body that immediate action should be taken. All this is very primitive as it ensured the survival of our prehistoric ancestors. For this reason, emotions are not under our control—which is something we should all be much aware of. As soon as the brain perceives danger, it springs into action to get the body ready to defend itself. This is without us knowing what the brain is doing, sometimes not understanding why we experience certain emotions and anxieties.

Your Health Is Important Too

Anxiety caused by unresolved issues related to emotions will keep on harming our physical and mental well-being until we do something about it. Emotions need to be recognized and acknowledged, and instead of undermining them, we should examine them. Consider questioning yourself: *Why do I feel this way? What caused this emotion? Is the emotion good or bad? Are there any issues surrounding the emotion? What can I do to remedy the issue?*

While negative emotions can cause harm to your overall well-being, positive emotions can bring healing.

Sensitives feel the need from a young age to hide their true self, which also adds to problems when it comes to their physical and mental well-being. School is supposed to be a place of safety and care, but for some, going to school can be a nightmare. Stress and anxiety experienced at a young age can cause future issues physically and mentally. Many sensitives who are still children experience rejection by parents, friends, teachers, and family members. Therefore, we should start by educating young people about sensitives and how the environment affects them. Teach people to love these sensitive children, so they can grow up to be a productive and innovative part of their community. However, sensitives can be productive and innovative without needing to "fit in." The fault is not in their sensitivity but in the non-sensitives' lack of education and information. All sensitives should embrace their individuality and live a life that works for them.

While psychotherapists have started to acknowledge the part emotions play in our well-being, it does not receive enough attention in mainstream care. It would be undoubtedly beneficial to include education on emotions and how to handle them when it comes to practices and institutions such as psychology, social care, and medical schools. Some people judge themselves or others because of emotions that are experienced. Teaching people that emotions aren't under their control would be a good place to start. People would feel less guilty or judgmental when it comes to emotions.

People who are educated and provided with tools to deal with emotions experience an enormous difference and improvement in their well-being. By allowing themselves to experience emotions, some become aware of physical healing taking place, such as healing of the stomach or intestines. Understanding that anger is also a normal emotional reaction can help people validate it when they feel angry, which would make it easier to deal with. Skills can be acquired on how to release anger without harming themselves or others. By practicing self-compassion, feelings of humiliation, self-pity, or self-loathing will be minimized.

These helpful skills will especially be beneficial to sensitives, who would first have to determine the source of the emotion before dealing with it. Remember, some sensitives can pick up on the emotions of others, absorb them, and make them their own. Realizing that the source of an experienced emotion is external may make it easier to deal with. When you allow yourself to experience all of your emotions without critique or judgment, they will simply pass after you have experienced them. Working with your emotions like this will change the firing pattern of the vagus nerve, reducing anxiety and helping your body to heal.

As one in five people are sensitive, highly sensitive, or empathic, it would be a good idea to adjust workplaces and the overall environment to suit their needs. This will prevent ailments such as chronic muscle tension, high blood pressure, insomnia, irritable bowel syndrome, migraines, infectious diseases, and mental health problems. If you are a sensitive, I'm sure you'll agree that people need to be educated to understand your sensitivity and the way your body and brain work, which can help you feel less embarrassed and ashamed. You can't live up to unreasonable expectations if your central nervous system does not allow it.

Managing emotions such as anger and hostility will improve your heart's health. Men, for example, who have anger issues are more likely to suffer cardiac effects such as heart attacks. Dealing with negative emotions can help alleviate other health issues such as the constriction of peripheral blood vessels, increased heart rate, unhealthy blood lipids, and hypertension. While experiencing bad emotions, your blood pressure rises, but every time you recall what has happened and you revisit the emotion, your blood pressure spikes again. Anger appears in different forms, which should all be dealt with. Anger can manifest as irritability, impatience, and grouchiness, which all have the potential of damaging your health.

Positive emotions cause the release of beneficial hormones and neurochemicals. Have you ever wondered why you feel better after you have cried? While you are crying, your body is flushing out the stress hormone present in your body. When you feel grateful, more oxygen is distributed among your cells which speeds up healing and boosts your immune system. Did you know that being in love affects your body for up to a year? It boosts your level of nerve growth factor which improves your memory by restoring your nervous system.

Beta-endorphins are released when you watch a funny comedy, which improves your mood and accelerates healing. Expecting to be laughing reduces cortisol and adrenaline in your body, while laughter decreases your risk of having a heart attack. Understand the benefits of feeling good, and cultivate habits that bring about happy feelings.

Chapter 4:

The Power of the Psyche

Our minds are far more complex than we give them credit for. Internal mechanisms and chemical processes are all controlled by our brains—yet still, we can focus on other tasks that need to be done while thinking about other things, such as a person we like, or what we will have for lunch or dinner. Your brain creates a new channel for every new thing it needs to focus on. And your brain is smart enough to prioritize, categorize, and organize everything, from tasks to daily habits, to make your life experience better. Just like a computer, your brain needs to be programmed to fulfill all that is required of you.

Are You Being Programmed?

We live on a planet that has gravity, spinning around its own axis. Without us realizing it, this factor influences all of us and every other living being on this planet. When a child learns to walk, do they get up one day and start walking around? No, they don't. The process of learning how to walk is meticulous and can take quite some time. Children need to learn how to walk because of gravity. Have you ever thought about that? The act of standing on your legs and using them to move around is a process used to counteract the pull of gravity. Then, it takes some more time to master the art of walking before the child starts running.

Do you think adults who can walk around effortlessly have to focus on the act of walking? They don't have to, as the skill to walk is fully programmed into their minds. As more responsibilities and obligations are added, your mind is programming itself to enable you to do the associated tasks. One way of programming your mind is through learning. People have known that the brain is responsible for learning since ancient times. However, neuroscientists have only been able to see what happens in the brain as learning occurs. All kinds of experiments are done to understand more about the brain and its functions.

Luckily we have enough information to know what a brain looks like without having to crack open a skull. Your brain is a dense network of fibers, containing approximately 100 billion neurons. It has three different parts: the stem, cerebellum, and cerebrum. The brainstem connects the brain to the spinal cord, regulating functions such as heart rate, breathing, and balance. Imagine having to manually control your breathing all day! It would be impossible. The stem has a stalk-like appearance as it narrows down to connect to the spine. It regulates subconscious functioning by forwarding messages from the brain to the rest of the body.

The cerebellum is at the bottom near the back of the brain. It may be smaller than the cerebrum but is vital to your existence. Bodily functions that are required daily as well as habits are programmed into the cerebellum. It also assists with vision and eye movement. But did you know that it is not only your eyes and ears that help you maintain your balance? Your cerebellum has special sensors that pick up when your body is moving and getting out of balance. It then sends signals to your body, helping it to adjust so you can maintain your balance. This is why you sometimes regain your balance so quickly when you slip on the dance floor.

The cerebrum is the larger part of the brain where learning, reasoning, and memory occur. In other words, this is the most programmable part of the brain. Did you know that different parts of the cerebrum are programmed according to their function? These functions include short-term memory, long-term memory, reasoning abilities, speech, language, and the processing of sensory input. This flood of information is first stored as short-term memory in a volatile part of the brain. This is done by a network of neurons firing up, sending signals between synapses. A neural pathway is created and the action or information is stored as short-term memory.

This new information stored in the short-term memory is taken to the structural core, where it is compared to existing memories. This is not always completely accurate, as degradation of the neurons is something that happens. The action of comparing the memories is instant, sending signals across billions of neurons and transmitting messages between synapses. But because of degradation, some memories are incomplete. Our minds fabricate details sometimes to fill the missing parts. This is why you sometimes *remember* something different than your siblings.

Learning and memory, or programming, happen as the connection between neurons is strengthened or weakened. Memories or knowledge that are often recalled cause a strengthening of connections, while things that are pushed to the back have weakened connections. A connection can weaken so much over time that the memory or information disappears. It is actually something we are all familiar with. When we were in school, what was the best way to learn? By repeating information over and over again, we ensured that new information was embedded thoroughly.

Our programming starts at a young age. We are brought up in accordance with moral standards and beliefs. This in itself differs between cultures and even households. For example, in one household it is normal to greet one another in the morning, after work and school, and at night. In another household it is regarded as normal for each person to go their own way, speaking only when it is necessary, with no *hellos* or *goodbyes*, *good mornings* or *good nights*. If it seems unbelievable, trust me, I've seen families who live like this.

The beliefs of parents aren't necessarily accurate, true, or beneficial. I know adults who are overweight because their parents used to tell them not to leave any food on their plates. This belief stuck, and even as adults, they can't stop eating until there is nothing left on their plates. It takes counseling and hard work for a person to heal from these false beliefs, and often shadow work is required for complete healing. Luckily, all is not bad. We also learn values, morals, and important life lessons from our parents. From learning to walk and learning to talk, our brains are open hard drives to be programmed, ready to gather and process new information.

In school, children are given a lot of information—they have to learn things about different subjects, are taught how to behave, and are guided with morals on what is acceptable and what is not. Can any teacher or parent ever be perfect? No one can, right? But as children, we absorb all available information, and through several mental processes build our identity around the things we are taught. This leads to new behaviors, either good or bad. Good if the child wants to be obedient, bad if the child decides to be a little rebel.

As an adult, whenever your brain recognizes new behavior, neurons start to fire up immediately, sending messages between synapses. Why? Your brain is trying to understand what you are doing, why you are doing it, and whether or not this new behavior is dangerous. Let's look at an example. When you get out of bed in the morning, you get ready for work, get in your car, and drive to the office. Let's say you have had your car for several years now. Do you need to focus on how to turn the key in the ignition, handle the gears, use your indicators, or turn the steering wheel? Do you still need to think about which pedals to push to get certain results? No, these things have become a habit.

New behaviors and information cause new neural pathways to form. When you learned how to drive, your neurons fired up wildly, trying to understand what you were doing. The more you were driving, the stronger the connections became. Soon, the connections were strong enough so you didn't need to consciously think about it anymore. While you were learning, you were using the outer parts of the brain, especially the prefrontal cortex. A lot of energy was used to create these neural pathways.

Once the connections were strong enough, your brain understood that this is a safe behavior that will be repeated. Your brain then shifts control of this neural pathway to the basal ganglia, which is a part of the inner brain. Behaviors and information, such as following a familiar route to work, are managed by the basal ganglia. While behaviors activating the prefrontal cortex require a lot of energy, behaviors controlled by the basal ganglia require very little energy. This is your brain's way of saving mental energy. You can then rather use this energy for more important things, such as critical thinking or remembering your wife's birthday.

But what if a car suddenly swerves right in front of you? What happens? You hit the brakes and control the steering wheel in an effort to avoid an accident. This behavior is again controlled by the prefrontal cortex. The moment your brain realizes that something bad is happening, signals are sent to your body to react. This action requires a large amount of energy. See how effective the brain is? Having the basal ganglia control the behavior of driving your brain saves energy, making this energy available to avoid a collision.

But still, though complex, our brains are not perfect. Sometimes bad behaviors can also turn into habits, such as drinking or smoking. Habits are indeed another way we program our minds.

It takes time and effort to break bad habits, but replacing bad habits with good ones is indeed possible. During the process of shadow work, bad habits may surface. When you have identified these bad habits, you can use shadow work to bring about change and replace them with good habits. This is how you can use the power of your brain for the greater good.

The Impact of Your Mindset

The way your mind is programmed can have a tremendous influence on your mindset. A mindset is a set of notions, assumptions, or methods held by one or more people toward a person, people, an object, incident, environment, and anything else for that matter. Your mindset will determine how you behave toward a person, in a situation, or toward yourself. Your mind needs to be ready for shadow work, which means your mindset will affect how successful you'll be.

A mindset can either be highly beneficial or detrimental, depending on the type of mindset. This is especially true for sensitives. Past programming may induce prejudice, often because of self-loathing and aspects of the self that are suppressed into the shadow self. A person may not be aware that they are acting in a certain way because of their mindset. People of all ages should be educated about the power of a mindset and how it determines their quality of life. Your mindset does not only have an impact on yourself but also on those around you. The truth is, we don't have only one mindset at a time, but several. However, one of these mindsets will overpower the rest, determining your behavior and attitude. The different mindsets are:

Positive

A positive mindset is always trying to find positivity in every situation or person. A person with a positive mindset is grateful and likes to look at the bright side of things.

Negative

A negative mindset focuses on the bad side of things, believing that things cannot get better. A person with a negative mindset believes the worst about people and situations.

Growth

A growth mindset is centered on learning and experiencing new things. A person with a growth mindset is innovative and proactive.

Fixed

A fixed mindset does not like learning or growing. A person with a fixed mindset accepts everything as it is, believing that nothing can change about it, whether it is a person or a situation.

Optimistic

An optimistic mindset believes that everything will always turn out for the good. A person with an optimistic mindset will believe a person or situation has something to offer, no matter what.

Pessimistic

A pessimistic mindset always anticipates the worst outcome, catastrophizing or distrusting those around them. A person with a pessimistic mindset will try to convince others that ideas, goals, people, or situations are bad.

Realistic

A realistic mindset sees the good in things, but also the bad. A person with a realistic mindset will not try and deter others from doing what they feel they need to, but will make them aware of the pros and cons.

Unrealistic

An unrealistic mindset is often gullible and believes almost everything. A person with an unrealistic mindset will set goals that are not achievable or expect behavior and successes from others that are beyond their ability. They will often ignore warnings.

Finding Mindsets

Think about the eight mindsets explained above, and let's use a story as an example to identify mindsets:

> *Joe, Dave, Tony, and Brian are going on a week's vacation. They are excited, as they are planning to spend a week in a cabin in the woods. They have to drive quite a distance to get to the cabin. As they are driving, they are all excited, chatting the time away. They stop at a gas station, where Joe, Dave, and Tony go into the gas station's convenience store. Brian is set with the task of filling up the tank. Soon, they are all back in the car to continue their long drive. They turn up a road, now en route to the cabin. They are*

surrounded by tall trees and thick brush; the road they're on is a single, meandering path heading deeper into the woods.

As it begins to get dark, Joe notices that they have used up more than half of the gas. Immediately he complains, "I knew we weren't going to make it! I knew it was too far!"

Dave smiles and says, "Don't worry, we'll make it. Even if we have to get there on fumes."

Tony reassures them and says, "Besides, there are cans filled with gas at the cabin. If it is necessary, one of us can walk there and bring back the jerricans."

Joe is in shock. "What! You expect one of us to walk up there! It sure isn't gonna be me!"

Dave shrugs and says, "No prob, I'll go. It won't be that far."

Tony adds to the conversation by saying, "Luckily we have enough food if we have to spend the night beside the road."

Brian laughs and says, "Dudes! You know I filled up the tank, right? I also filled the two jerry cans I put in the trunk. So don't worry, we won't run out."

Everyone is relieved, especially Joe. He just watched one too many horror movies.

Now take some time and sort the list of mindsets according to the behaviors of the different characters. Which mindsets do you think fit with which character? Do this first before we continue. Have you done it? You'll only be doing yourself a favor.

It is clear that Joe's mindset is both negative, fixed, and pessimistic, right? But, he is also realistic, knowing that they won't be able to reach the cabin with the fuel they have.

Dave's mindset is positive and optimistic, but also unrealistic and fixed.

Tony's mindset is positive, growth, and optimistic, but with a touch of an unrealistic mindset.

Brian's mindset is pessimistic, positive, growth, and realistic. You may wonder why I state that he also has a pessimistic mindset. If he was optimistic, he would have decided that the fuel in their tank was enough to get them to the cabin, but he was pessimistic enough to worry something would go wrong, and filled the two jerricans.

Therefore, mindsets labeled as *bad* are not always bad. We need to have a negative or pessimistic mindset sometimes. For example, when a friend feels terribly sick, will you be optimistic and tell them they'll be fine, or will you be pessimistic and tell them they need to go and see a doctor? It is good to have the positive mindsets in charge, but we should allow the negative ones some space as well.

Your mindset will also determine how you will approach shadow work. If you are negative and pessimistic about it, it will never work. The great thing about a mindset is that it can be changed.

How do you change your mindset? By reprogramming your mind.

Reprogramming Your Mind

Your mindset and the way you think determine what your life will be like. Many people don't realize this and simply let life go by without being willing to change their perspective. How often have you thought about doing something great, but then just let it slip away without further consideration? This happens to millions of people all the time. Your brain is programmed to reflect everything familiar to you, constantly comparing new experiences with existing information. This means that your mind reflects everything you know about your environment. This begs the question—does your environment determine how you think, or does the way you think determine your environment?

If you go through a day performing the same habits you have been repeating for the last few years (such as getting up in the morning, getting ready for work, drinking coffee from your favorite mug, driving to work, doing what is expected of you at your workplace, and then return home to watch television, have supper, and then go to sleep), were there any changes to your way of thinking or your physical brain? You repeat daily the same actions that produce the same thoughts, coming with familiar frustrations you have to face every day. This means that what you are doing will constantly produce the same outcome.

This may make you feel safe and secure, but perhaps you have yearned for a change, something to happen, or things to get better. Your experiences every day activates circuits in your brain, which then leads to a certain kind of thinking, directly linked to your environment. As you do the same things and see the same people, your brain is creating a way of thinking that is already familiar to you. In other words, you are only thinking about the things you already know.

If you want things to change, especially if you are a sensitive, is to begin thinking bigger than your environment. Think about what you truly want and create a vision around it. All the great people are visionaries—people such as Joan of Arc, Albert Einstein, and William Wallace. When they had their visions, hopes, and dreams, did they perceive them literally? No, it was not something they could see, taste, or touch. Still, they had given their vision so much power that they started living as if their vision was already a reality. You and I have the same ability. We have the skills to create a vision, empower it, and live as if it is already a reality.

Your personality consists of three parts: how you feel, think, and act. This becomes your personal reality. The person you are, or your *personality*, has created your personal reality, which is the situation you are in at this moment—also known as *your life*. If you want to change your personal reality or your life, you will have to change the emotional connection you have about things, your thoughts, and your habits and behaviors. You can never create a new personal reality if you stick to the same personality. In some essence, you have to become someone different.

When you repeat the same actions every day, these actions are hard-wired into your brain. The neurons that fire up follow the same pathways every day, with impulses continually running among familiar roads. Your mind is how you use your brain, in other words, it's your brain in action. Even by reminding yourself who you are, your neurons are firing in the same pattern every time you do it. Behaviors become habits as the brain becomes familiar with the behaviors. Your brain does not only change mentally but physically as well. The neurological pathways are detectable, as these pathways create visible clues where the neurons fire up.

This means that to change your personality, you have to change your brain mentally and physically. How do you do that? By creating new combinations, patterns, and sequences. This will cause your brain to work in a different way than it is used to. And don't worry, your brain can handle it! How did we become who we are? We did it by absorbing information and knowledge from a young age. As an adult, you can still use information and knowledge to create new pathways and change the physiology of your brain. Every time you learn a new thing, such as a skill, your brain is immediately creating new connections.

When you recall information, you are sustaining and maintaining those new connections. When you entertain a new thought, neurons fire. Yes, just by consciously thinking about something, the neurons begin creating pathways. When this happens, a different part of your brain is activated, which releases certain chemicals, creating an emotion that is linked to what you are thinking. This is true for either positive or negative thinking. Positive thinking can summon joyous emotions, while negative thinking can cause anxiety, stress, or depression.

Ultimately, the chemicals enter your body, and you have feelings associated with your thoughts. Feeling good can lead to positive thinking while feeling bad leads to negative thinking. But regardless of the way you think, it becomes a loop. You begin to feel the way you think and think the way you feel. Emotions and thoughts begin feeding one another, which can be either to your benefit or can be detrimental to your physical and emotional health. See the importance of shadow work? By eliminating negative thinking and beliefs, you will be reducing a lot of chemicals that only serve to make you feel worse.

Once your thoughts and feelings are aligned, you enter a state of "being." Thoughts are used by your brain to communicate, while your body communicates through feelings. According to Doctor Joe Dispenza, up to 95% of the behaviors performed by an adult who is 35 years old are automated habits. This means that most of an adult's day consists of basically mindless activities that don't require high levels of thinking. Only 5% of your conscious mind is used for new and unfamiliar activities (FightMediocrity, 2019). This is why we sometimes have a great thought, but feelings of unworthiness or self-loathing stop us from following through. This happens when a person's body is not aligned with positive thinking, meaning that the person is filled with negativity.

Such negativity can prevent a person from achieving the life they desire. The negativity quickly overturns any possible positive thoughts, keeping the person trapped in their negative state of being. But people should know, it should be shouted from the rooftops—we all have the power to overturn this negativity! We have the ability to change! We *can* change our programming! We don't need to be content with a way of thinking; many people only bring about change after being faced with trauma or some other terrifying experience.

But why should anyone wait for something horrible to happen? We all can do something about it now. You can decide to take back your life this instant—refusing negativity, and becoming filled with hope for what shadow work can do for you. Don't think of shadow work as something you *have* to do. Think of it as something you *get* to do. Reprogram your mind. Think about those millions who don't get the chance, those who haven't received the good news. Be grateful, do shadow work, and then reach out to those who need you.

Chapter 5:

First-Aid for Your Soul

In this chapter, you will find methods to deal with aspects of your shadow self whenever you are overcome with emotions such as anxiety, stress, or fear. The methods are creative and focused on honoring your sensitivity, helping you release negative energy in a kind and easy way. Although these methods are not particularly focused entirely on shadow work such as the guided meditation in Chapter 2, they can be used during shadow work. These tools are efficient in helping you deal with overwhelming emotions that you might face during shadow work. All these methods are effective, especially for sensitives. Some of the tools overlap in their benefit to mind, body, and spirit, but are categorized in this Chapter according to their main focus.

Some methods of shadow work make use of shadow work journal prompts. These are confronting questions that prompt you to think about things that may stress you out. For sensitives, this method is not always effective. It can cause a heightened sense of unease as these prompts can require you to be too confronting or get in touch directly with something too painful. In this book, you won't find this method. Our guided meditation takes a more gentle approach, especially for sensitives.

Tools to Heal Your Body

There are several tools you can use for the healing of your body. We will be focusing on the physical cleansing of negative energy.

Wash Away the Stress

Bathing may be something you do daily, but are you truly aware of its benefits? Perhaps you prefer to take a shower? Try switching the shower with a bathtub sometime. Don't rush it, as enjoying a prolonged session of relaxation in a warm bathtub will loosen your muscles and ease pain. As you are relaxing, you'll experience a delightful decrease in stress, tension, and negativity. Not only will you feel physically clean, but also refreshed. Don't just take a bath to get clean, though. You can use the warm water as an object of focus as a technique of meditation. As you are relaxing, be aware of the warmth of the water. Feel yourself relaxing. Experience the warmth against your skin and feel your muscles relaxing. As a sensitive, it is easy to become overstimulated. Bathing is a very easy and relaxing way of restoring the senses and regaining mental balance.

Taking a bath—something so simple yet so very effective.

Use Mudras

This practice involves using hand gestures to direct energy flow throughout your body. It is a type of yoga that can help you become more spiritually aware. One of the most potent mudras is the *Abhaya Mudra*. You can use this as a tool if you feel the need for safety, protection, confidence, and strength. Many use this mudra to protect themselves from negative energy and harm as well as to reduce anxiety and stress, as it calms the nervous system. The action involved during this mudra is simple. Sit down comfortably and raise your right hand to shoulder height, letting your palm face forward.

This same method is seen in Buddhist depictions that are centuries old. The ancients had a great understanding of energy and how to maintain a calm nervous system. The great thing is that mudras work for everyone, regardless of culture or religion, and you can do them anywhere, anytime. Mudras can come in handy when you feel overwhelmed and have a chance to take a quick break, such as from a conference or meeting.

Get Moving

We all know that exercise is beneficial to both the mind and the body, yet too many of us neglect this important practice. Exercising is not only good for your health but can help uplift your mood. While exercising, endorphins are released making you feel calm and happy. Also, it helps you feel energized and relaxed as it flushes the stress hormone out of your body. There are many different exercises you can try. If you are new to this, try walking as an exercise. You can start by walking at a normal pace, then, as you become more fit and accustomed to walking, you can begin to increase the pace without causing too much impact on your joints, if that is what you are worried about. Walking can help clear negative emotions and thoughts.

Yoga is another low-impact exercise that works wonders. It helps in alleviating tension, negativity, and stress. By doing yoga you are strengthening your core muscles, improving your flexibility, and promoting your overall well-being. Did you know that on

YouTube you can find a lot of yoga practices specially designed for sensitives?

The Therapy in Smiling

When should we smile? When things are great? When we get a promotion, a gift, or a surprise? Sure, we would smile *then*, but by limiting our smiles to certain occasions we are also limiting ourselves. Do you know why it feels so good to smile? When you smile, endorphins are released, eliminating negative emotions, stress, and thoughts, making you feel happy. What a quick and easy way to get a boost! When was the last time you smiled? Have you ever tried smiling at yourself? Go to a mirror, look at yourself, and smile. Smile in celebration of who you are. Then, say out loud: *I love you!*

> *Peace begins with a smile.* –Mother Teresa

Eat Well, Be Well

It is no secret that the food we eat affects us mentally and physically. We really *are* what we eat. By keeping your diet nutritious and healthy you maintain a healthy and sharp mind and provide your body with the energy it requires for adequate functioning. Healthy foods, such as dark green leafy foods, can help remove negative energy from your body. Consuming food and drinks that contain things such as refined sugar, alcohol, and caffeine may give you a temporary boost, but as your blood sugar level crashes, you will feel fatigued and listless. Fried and processed foods and excessive animal proteins can leave you feeling bloated and drained of energy.

Opt for healthier choices such as beans, whole grains, vegetables, fruit, nuts, and seeds. As sensitives have to deal with overwhelming emotions and unwanted energies often, they need their minds to be clear, their bodies to be energized, and negative energy to be removed. Eating the right food is one way of achieving this. Besides, healthy food can be fun and delicious, which means you can enjoy it while eating and continue to enjoy its benefits after. Some people argue that it is impossible to eat healthy food, as it is either too expensive or takes too long to prepare. However, healthier options don't need to be expensive. If you are interested in a healthier diet, research the types of food that are affordable and within your reach. You may be surprised when you see you don't need to expand your budget drastically for healthier food options. Many healthy dishes are quick and easy to prepare. There are several books and other sources available for quick, easy, and affordable healthy foods you can enjoy.

Crystals—It's Not Magic, It's Science!

Have you noticed that crystals each have their unique shape? Quarts grow as pointed shapes, while galena develops into cubes. It all comes down to their atoms and how they are arranged. The atoms of crystals form a unique pattern that is repeated continuously, according to the crystal type. However, it is not only crystals that have this method of atom formation. Chocolate, sugar, ice, sand, and DNA all have crystalline structures. All atoms vibrate at a specific frequency, meaning crystals vibrate at their own frequencies. This is why the ancients believed that crystals can be used for various reasons, such as healing, clarity, and relaxation.

According to Doctor David Hamilton, crystals work in three different ways. The first property crystals have, such as quartz crystals, is *diamagnetism*. This means that the crystal is interfering with the Earth's magnetic field, in that the magnetic field bends around the crystal. Anything close to the crystal receives its normal magnetism, added with the deflected magnetism from the crystal.

Research done at the California Institute of Technology proved that the Earth's magnetic field can make a difference in people's brainwaves. People were placed in an electromagnetic-shielded room in which the Earth's magnetic field was replicated. They then tweaked the magnetic field by rotating the direction of its flow. Although the people in the room were unaware that the magnetic field had rotated, all of the participants' brainwaves abruptly changed. This proves that our brains are sensitive to magnetic fields.

Doctor Hamilton also explains that clear crystals can be used to achieve mental clarity. The person holding the crystal gazes at how clear it is, creating a mental milestone such as, *I want my mind to be as clear as this crystal.* Doctor Harrison claims that this is an effective way to clear your mind, as the crystal is used as a mental representation.

Crystals can also be used in color psychology. Colors influence how people think, act, and behave. Think about marketing, especially when you enter a retail store. What do they use to attract people and potential shoppers? They use colors. Studies have found that the color *red* entices people to buy more, while soft blue lights have a calming effect. In the same way, crystals can be used to attain a certain mental state and to change behavior (Lawrence, 2021). If you are thinking about using crystals, just keep searching. You will be drawn to the crystal or crystals you need. Everyone reacts differently to crystals, but when you shop online you can search the internet for "crystals for highly sensitive persons". It will make it easier to find crystals that match your needs.

Healing for Your Soul

In this section, we'll be looking at tools you can use to heal your mind. Your mind should never be neglected. It is the determining factor of how you will live your life.

Breathe In, Breathe Out

We have all watched talent shows featuring nervous contestants. What is one of the first things the judges often say? They tell the contestant to take deep breaths to calm their nerves. It's a fact—taking deep breaths helps you to concentrate, focus, relax, and calm down. Deeper breaths cause more oxygen to flow through your bloodstream and help to clear negative energy. Breathing techniques are often used in yoga and meditation. It removes negative thoughts and emotions, uplifts your mood, and increases positive energy. *Kapalabhati Pranayama* is an ancient practice used to generate energy in the body and helps with circulation and digestion.

Breathing exercises are very easy and doable. Many people underestimate its effectiveness because of its simplicity. Don't let this opportunity for overall improvement pass you by. Take time during the day to do some breathing exercises. This exercise may be simple but will surprise you with its effectiveness.

If you are a sensitive, these exercises will be very beneficial when it comes to shadow work. During shadow work, you'll need tools for keeping calm and relaxed. Breathing exercises should be at the top of your list. Overall, sensitives are susceptible to stress and anxiety which can impair breathing. This means that many sensitives lack sufficient oxygen for optimal bodily and mental functioning. Oxygen plays a big part in cell regeneration, which means that sensitives suffer from cell depletion.

Toxins that accumulate in the body cannot be flushed out while a person is in an anxious state, which is why sensitives struggle with a build-up of toxins as well. Lack of sleep is also harmful, as cell and organ regeneration takes place while we are sleeping. Sensitives battling anxiety often struggle with insomnia as well. Breathing exercises are the key to calming the nervous system and restoring all bodily functions and processes.

Let's do a little experiment to show how effective deep breathing is. Sit down comfortably and close your eyes. Are you ready? Imagine that you are in the wrong place at the wrong time. A house was just broken into and you just happen to be walking by. The police mistakenly think that you are the burglar. They shove you against a wall and place you in handcuffs, then escort you to the back of their vehicle where they unceremoniously throw you on the back seat. You try to plead your innocence, but it falls on deaf ears.

Now imagine that you are driven to a police station, then thrown into a jail cell. You are surrounded by criminals. You end up sitting in a corner, hoping that everyone will leave you alone. Can you feel the tightness in your chest? How do you feel overall? Open your eyes, and then close them again. Get comfortable and take deep breaths. Breathe in and hold your breath for three seconds, then breathe out for three seconds. Keep on repeating this until you feel calm and relaxed, emotionally and physically.

Remember—don't try any new types of exercise, methods, or tools before discussing them with your physician. Your health status is just as unique as you are. Something that works for one person will not necessarily work for another. Always put safety above curiosity.

Learn to Detach

Have you ever known someone, but your friendship or relationship had run its course? Your connection no longer serves any purpose. Yet, just as you start to cut the cord from this person, they contact you. Why does this happen? They can detect the cord being cut. However, if your relationship with this person truly serves no purpose, or if this was a person who caused you harm or weighed you down, cut that cord for good. Don't pity them or allow them back into your life. Only allow attachments with those who lift you up and where relationships have a fulfilling purpose.

Sensitives often sacrifice themselves for the happiness or contentment of others. We are surprised at how *selfish* or *rude* other people can be. However, I think we often mistake selfishness or rudeness with personal boundaries. There is no shame in placing a boundary. If you know that a boundary is required, place it. If you feel bad about it, allow the emotion, process it, and move on. When these emotions are not processed, they can end up becoming part of your shadow.

Smoke-Out Your Blues

Smoke cleansing (specifically known as "smudging" *only* for those of indigenous heritage) involves lighting a small corner of a herb, such as sage, mugwort, or sandalwood, and blowing it out. This allows the herb to release smoke while smoldering slowly. It is an ancient practice used to clear negative energy from specific places and people. To keep the herbs and ashes contained, you can use a holder such as a large ashtray. This will help the ash to remain intact. Some people like to use a plate or a large clamshell. To distribute the smoke, you can use your hand or a large feather. Start with the crown of your head, distributing the smoke, until you reach the soles of your feet. Concentrate on the cleansing power, visualizing the negative energy dispersing and being replaced with positive energy. There is a science to smoke cleansing with proven benefits, which is why it has continued to be such a popular practice through the ages.

Can My Spirit Become Sick?

Just like your mind and body, your spirit can be unwell too. In this section, we'll be concentrating on tools you can use to heal your spirit. You don't need to be a spiritual person for this to be effective. In psychology, the spirit is often referred to as a person's core beliefs, attitude, and core identity. False beliefs, toxic environments, narcissistic family members or friends (among many other things) can slowly poison your spirit, filling you with negative energy. Let's get spiritual!

Purifying Your Aura

I have come across some people who do not believe that all living things have an aura. To them, the idea of an aura is too mystical and they see it as a bunch of "hocus pocus." But, in fact, we all do have auras. It is an energy field existing around our physical bodies which can be observed. Beverly Rubik from the Institute for Frontier Research in Oakland, Calif, uses a digital Kirlian camera to photograph people's auras. Your aura can be affected negatively by experiences, such as past trauma, bad life choices, or bad relationships. In the same way, your aura can also be affected by positive experiences.

How can you tell if your aura is charged with negative energy? There are several symptoms, including feeling exhausted without explanation, feeling that you don't belong, clumsiness, frustration, and disconnected emotions. A positively charged aura is radiant, attracts people, and makes you feel loved, appreciated, grateful and warm.

You can use the following method to cleanse your aura:

Sit quietly and comfortably, focusing on your breathing—in through your nose, out through your mouth. Every time you inhale, visualize white light entering your body. Allow the light to flow throughout your body. Imagine the light as pure and peaceful energy. Every time you breathe out, visualize black smoke being exhaled. Watch as it leaves your body and your energy field. Imagine the black smoke dissolving into the air or ground. Keep on visualizing the white light as it flows and fills every inch of your body. See how it glows, bright and white, banishing the black smoke. Repeat the visualization of the white light until it has filled your entire body and you feel a change. By the end, you should feel lighter and unburdened.

Miraculous Meditation

As we have seen in Chapter 2, meditation is an essential tool for sensitives. You can use this method to strengthen your intuition and acquire inner wisdom. Sensitives need to maintain a calm and healthy mind; meditation helps you to de-stress and alleviate anxiety, helping to battle the feeling of becoming overwhelmed. This will also improve your overall mood and perspective. Meditating frequently can help you disconnect from your environment, especially if your environment generates negative energy and stress. Meditation helps your mind to quiet down and opens doors to new opportunities. *Mantra meditation* is powerful in that it cleanses your spirit and revitalizes your energy. It also helps if you feel that energy is blocked by clearing out these blockages from your chakras. Meditation has a lot of proven benefits. Currently, between 200 and 500 million people practice meditation worldwide.

A *mantra* is a word or phrase that you repeat, either by saying or singing it. Meditation techniques make use of different mantras. There are countless options, but the mantra you should be using is one relevant to your life. Seek out a mantra or mantras that make a difference in your life. Whenever you speak or sing a mantra, listen to the words and understand their meaning. Believe in these words. Absorb their energy and in that way, you empower yourself.

Develop an Attitude of Gratitude

We all know the word *gratitude*, but do we truly understand what it means? It is a bit cliché when you tell someone to be grateful for something because others don't have it. But, cliché or not, it is true. I recently watched a video of a 57-year-old man who received EnChroma glasses as a gift. I could barely contain my emotions as this man burst into tears. He cried because of joy. I cried for his joy, but also for my ingratitude. This man has lived for 57 years without the ability to distinguish colors. I have been able to distinguish colors all my life, yet, I am guilty of taking it for granted. You can watch the video on YouTube. Search for "James Receives Pilestone Colorblind Glasses for His 57th Birthday."

It broke my heart when the man looked up at the trees. That was the moment he burst into tears. Here I am, walking among beautiful trees every day, not even noticing it anymore. But for this man the beauty of the trees was overwhelming. I immediately chose to feel more gratitude. Every time I see something colorful, I feel gratitude building in my heart, thinking of all those millions of people who can't enjoy it.

When you have gratitude, you are surrounded by a shield of positivity. Gratitude helps you to remain humble, grounded, and calm, even when you are faced with challenges or negativity. I have found that gratitude is the one thing that helps to counteract an unhealthy ego. Gratitude attracts nothing else than positive energy to you and your life. Make it a part of your morning and nighttime routine. In the morning, write down one, two, or three things you are grateful for. At night, before you go to bed, read what you have written, and see if you can add more things to the list. Perhaps something happened to you during the day that stirred your gratitude? If so, write it down.

Be Mindfully Kind

As a sensitive, how does it feel when you are kind toward another person or display an act of kindness? It makes you feel good, doesn't it? Acts of kindness can cleanse you from negative energy, filling you with positive instead. Decide to be kinder through acts such as smiling at strangers, giving compliments where they are due, giving hugs to those who need them, holding doors open, and writing notes of inspiration and gratitude for your friends. But perhaps even more importantly, decide to be kinder to *yourself*. You will need this while doing shadow work. Snuff the negative self-talk and compliment yourself. Treat yourself to a day in the park, a massage, or a good movie. Realize that you are most deserving of your own kindness. Did you know that self-hugging is a real and fun thing with serious benefits? Go on, just try it!

Bells, Chimes, and the Soothing Sound of Water

I'm sure you have heard of *feng shui* before. Do you make use of *feng shui*? You should. Just like mantras, meditation, and mudras, *feng shui* is an ancient art developed by the Chinese to improve the flow of energy, creating harmony between a person and their environment. The words *feng* means wind, and *shui* means water. This means that the elements wind and water are essential in maintaining a positive flow of energy. The ringing of bells and wind chimes causes vibrations that help to align energies, improving the flow of positive energy.

If something left bad energy in your home such as an argument, you can ring a handheld bell to realign the energy, so the negative energy can flow out and positive energy flow back in. You can use singing bowls and yoga chimes to clear and align your chakras and shift energies. Some meditators like to use music while they are meditating. If you choose to use such music, it should preferably be instrumental, or with minimal voices. Music with lyrics can distract you and cause your session to be unsuccessful.

Fountains and water features also have a soothing effect. Have you ever sat close to a fountain or water feature after a hard day's work? How did the sound of the water make you feel? If you haven't experienced this yet, give it a try. Don't just *hear* the water—*listen* to it. Feel it. Be fully aware of the sound it makes. Sound is a powerful way of dealing with energies, as we will learn in the next chapter.

Chapter 6:

Using Sound and Smell

In this Chapter, we will be examining the efficacy of music and dancing as a tool to ease shadow work.

I know most people who are sensitives are shy and reserved, but don't worry, you won't be dancing in front of a crowd. You can use these tools in the privacy of your home. Later, we'll also discuss how you can use smell as a tool. Your senses can be harnessed to make your experience of shadow work less challenging and more of an adventure.

The Power of Music

Every great movie has a beautiful and striking original score. Why do movie producers carefully pick the people who will create and conduct this music? They know that a good original soundtrack will greatly improve the quality of the movie. Have you ever thought about the score of your favorite movies? I suggest that you try an experiment. Try watching your favorite movie (or at least one of your favorites), but after watching an action or other dramatic scene, turn down the volume completely and watch the scene again. Does it have the same feeling? Does it excite you as much as it did when you could hear the accompanying music? My guess is that it won't.

A movie score is carefully orchestrated to fit with every scene. Imagine a romantic scene where the guy and girl share their first kiss, but the background music is linked to a chase scene from

Terminator. It won't fit at all and will confuse your brain completely. Music has the power to create any mood the film producers want. That is just the power of music—it is a universal language that can turn your emotions in an instant. Many people, when they have their hearts broken, listen to songs about break-ups and lost love. Those who have just fallen in love will listen to appropriate love songs. Why? Because people have been using music as a way to change their moods for centuries, if not millennia.

Sensitives are drawn to music. With some music, we as sensitives can truly feel the heart and emotions of the composer while we listen to their work. I often feel like I'm finding hidden messages in some types of music. Such music can often bring me to tears as I marvel at its beauty. And I have to admit that it sometimes frustrates me when another person listens to this music, and it does nothing for them. For a sensitive, this can be both a blessing and a burden. We see and hear things non-sensitives don't. Still, I feel that any person can receive the fullness of bliss that comes with good music. If your heart is open, it can receive. Music can reach deep where the spoken word cannot.

Does Music Have the Ability to Heal?

According to Markham Heid (2018) research has shown that music can help a person maintain their mood and alleviate depression. Listening to music can also increase blood flow by reducing cholesterol. It can reduce the level of hormones secreted because of stress and anxiety, ease pain, and aid in a successful recovery after an operation. When you listen to the right music, neurons fire and can gradually restructure your brain in areas associated with attention, memory, the regulation of emotions, and ensuring that you have a positive mood. It also activates specific neurochemical processes focused on positivity and enhancement.

In 2016, Kim Innes, a professor of epidemiology at West Virginia University's School of Public Health, took part in a study focused on the effect of music on older people who are dealing with cognitive decline. They found that music has the potential to reduce stress and improve their mood and overall well-being. In this study, a comparison was made between the effects of listening to music and meditating. They found that there were many similar results, such as an improvement in quality of sleep and overall mood. This means that listening to music and meditation both have the potential to be powerful tools that can be used for emotional and physical healing. Even so, I suggest that you do not swap one for the other. See it this way—you have two easy practices that can serve as powerful tools to aid in your healing, music and meditation.

However, music that is slower in tempo, has longer notes, and has gradual chord progressions are more suited for inducing a calming effect. With this being said, some people claim that listening to heavy metal or hard rock music has a calming effect on them. This implies that all people do not react the same to the same kind of music. If you are interested in using music as a tool for healing, you need to find music that has a calming effect on you. Some people like to have their heartbeats elevated and feel emotionally charged, but that is not relaxing. Just because you favor a type of music doesn't mean it can be used as a tool for healing. Physical and mental healing can only come from a state of relaxation and a calm mind.

Professor of psychology Daniel Levitin at the McGill University in Canada, states that music activates every mapped part of the human brain. Indeed, music *is* a universal language. It has the power to bypass rational thought and reach the places where we have buried our suppressed aspects—our shadow self. As sensitives become overwhelmed easily, they are more susceptible to stress and anxiety. When a person experiences stress, their body produces cortisol, which is also known as the "stress hormone."

A prolonged period of being exposed to excess cortisol will cause the person to feel exhausted and induce a state of fight, flight, or freeze. When a person is under even longer exposure to this state, it can lead to mental health issues, such as chronic anxiety, depression, or chronic pain. Listening to soothing music, such as classical or ambient music, reduces the levels of cortisol, thereby reducing levels of anxiety and stress. Music also has a positive effect when used for the treatment of mental health. People who take some time to listen to soothing music are less likely to experience burnout, even with a busy schedule.

Amazingly, people who listen to music through headphones while under anesthesia have lower cortisol levels while being operated on. This improves their post-operation healing process. Were you aware of this amazing power that is right at your fingertips? Well, now you are, so don't excuse it, use it.

Dive Into Dancing

While soothing music is required (at least for most people) to calm their minds and relax their bodies, we can release negative energy through dancing, which requires music that excites and invigorates. Shadow work often deals with unwanted emotional baggage, things that we hold on to that are of no benefit to us, such as false beliefs, fears, trauma, and bad habits. This emotional baggage only accumulates as we go through life if we have no way of getting rid of it. It does not only affect us mentally, but physically as well. We are in danger of falling into a loop, or a downward detrimental spiral, as being physically stagnant leads to a stagnant state of mind, and having a stagnant state of mind can lead to being physically stagnant. Why? Because being stagnant causes blockages in the flow of energy.

To get rid of emotional baggage, you need an effective tool. Movement is a perfect tool to achieve emotional freedom. It is near impossible to force yourself mentally to get rid of negative thoughts and emotions. This is why movement is the perfect tool.

While several meditations use movement, you can rid yourself of negative energy through dancing. No rituals, lessons, or professionality is required. All you need is a body and music— and of course, the will to get rid of negative energy. As your movements will be based on your intuition, you don't need to worry about how you move or how good you look while you're dancing.

Assess Yourself Mentally and Physically

Before you start dancing, you need a baseline to measure your progress. Think about how you are feeling physically, emotionally, and mentally. If you want, you can write it down, either on a piece of paper or in a dance journal. I suggest you use a journal, so you can always go back and see how far you have progressed over a month, year, or a couple of years.

Pick Your Groove to Move

Which songs make you feel excited and energized? Do you have a favorite playlist you use at lively parties? Choose a song or a playlist of songs.

This Sensitive's on Fire!

Listen to the music you have chosen. How does it make you feel? Do you feel the energy and excitement building up? If so, then good. You're on the right track.

Slave to the Music

This step is the most fun—let go and just dance! Don't think of how good you are. In fact, don't think about what you are doing at all. Let your body move intuitively. Your body will tell you how it wants to move to get rid of negative energy. Follow its prompts, even if it means shaking your leg like a wet dog. Expect the unexpected—*anything* can happen. This kind of dancing can easily release emotions like tears or laughter. Once, after dancing for a long time, I even entered a blissful state of oneness. Try it. I guarantee that you won't regret it.

If you have friends or there are people in your neighborhood who practice ecstatic dancing, invite them over once in a while and have an ecstatic party. Ecstatic dancing is becoming more popular globally. When dancing along with other people, more energy is gathered, and therefore, more negativity can be released. It's all about shared intent. Just go with the flow and follow the music... and not any rules.

Go Wild for Five Minutes

To make this practice efficient, you should dance for no less than five minutes. You can dance for a while longer if you feel the need to, but five minutes of dancing every day is already an amazing tool for removing negative energy.

Be Mindful of Your Body

Take a moment to feel gratitude toward your body. Focus on how thankful you are that dancing is something you can do. Bathe yourself in the glow of your gratitude.

Do Another Assessment

Take a moment to think about how you feel, physically and mentally. Don't think about what you have written before you have started. Focus on how you are feeling now, right after your session of dancing. Do you notice any changes? Write down how you feel on the next page of your dance journal. Now, compare your entries. What did five minutes of dancing do for you?

It is such a simple practice, yet so effective. For optimal results, you should make a habit of dancing every day. If you can't for whatever reason, try dancing when you feel irritable and negative. The moment you feel a blockage in your flow of energy, turn on the music and start moving.

Get Ecstatic

Ecstatic dancing is the method described before in this section. It is dancing without thinking, allowing your body to guide you. Though dancing has been present since ancient times across the world, it is used mostly for entertainment today. Who would have thought that dancing can help with ailments and even make shadow work less challenging? Now that we know, there's no stopping our groovy moves!

The Story of Petra Biro

Few things are as inspirational as hearing a testimony from a fellow sensitive. This is the story of Petra Biro, a sensitive ballet dancer who found healing in dancing.

Petra started dancing at the age of six. She always considered dancing to be a way of communication. Although she was shy, she found that dancing was a way in which she could fearlessly express herself. To her, dancing was a natural thing to do. That was until she enrolled at a professional ballet school. She found the exams to be extremely tough, and also had a hard time coming to terms with the fact that she wasn't perfect. At that time, she was not aware that she was a sensitive. Sensitives are kind and gentle toward others but can be harsh, critical, and perfectionistic toward themselves. This made her feel lonely. She had to deal with all this on her own.

Being a sensitive also had its perks—she was easily able to connect with the music. Petra was able to memorize choreographies easily, and also found it easy to stay within the beats of the music without the need to count them (as many ballet dancers do). It was then that she realized dancing holds a multitude of benefits, not only for ballet dancers but for anyone who takes the time to dance, professionally or not. Petra found that dancing improves balance, flexibility, cardiovascular health, attention, concentration, physical strength, spatial awareness, and reduces stress. Wow, that's a lot of benefits! So, let's take it from a professional: Dancing is good for you—whether you practice your secret living-room ballet moves or not.

Essential Oils

Similar to sound, other senses can also be used to change your mood. The sense of smell is an effective tool for mood enhancement. For years, real estate agents have been using the trick of placing freshly baked cookies in the kitchen whenever they have an open house. Movie cinemas use both colors and smell to attract people and entice them into buying snacks and drinks. What is the first thing you smell as you enter the cinema? What else other than popcorn? Some people who don't want to spend more money will either eat something before going to watch a movie or opt for something cheap. However, just as many people give in to the smell of fresh popcorn and end up buying it anyway. Chances are they'll buy even more snacks.

Or what about when you go to your grandmother's house and you smell her cooking? How does it make you feel? I can even mention the smell of rain, or the tilled earth just after the rain. There are so many examples of how smell can change anyone's mood. In this section, we'll be talking about essential oils—an essential part of healing during shadow work.

Soothing Your Soul During Shadow Work

Sensitives are prone to be kind toward nature, and nature shows her gratitude by being kind to us. There are several essential oils that provide healing and relaxation, especially for sensitives. Some oils can be used specifically during the course of shadow work. In this section, we'll look at essential oils you can use when certain fears embedded in your shadow self come into the light.

Insecurity

Feeling insecure can cause you to avoid trying new things, as your mind is trying to keep you in familiar areas and away from the unknown. This inhibits dreaming and setting goals that can improve your life and make it amazing. Escape feelings of insecurity by using oils such as marjoram, clary sage, neroli, and lavender.

Powerlessness

Feeling powerless can be very crippling, as it causes you to underestimate your own abilities. Feelings of powerlessness can be remedied by using oils such as yuzu, peppermint, rosemary, and cedarwood.

Disapproval

Fearing disapproval can cause you to seek approval from any possible source. This can lead to you becoming a slave to a narcissist or manipulative person. You can completely lose your own identity in an effort to please others, simply for their approval. You can fend off the fear of disapproval by using essential oils such as chamomile, grapefruit, sandalwood, and bergamot.

Unworthiness

Feeling unworthy can cause us to miss out on many opportunities, as we feel we are not worthy of unexpected chances or new possibilities. You can combat feelings of unworthiness with the aromas of patchouli, jasmine, ylang-ylang, and rose geranium.

Helplessness

Having a fear of not being in control can cause a lot of stress and anxiety. An overwhelming and prolonged feeling of helplessness—that there is nothing that can be done to help the situation—can easily lead to an anxiety disorder. You can take back control of your life and fight this fear by using aromas such as myrrh, frankincense, geranium, and rose.

As you can see, there is a myriad of essential oils and aromas that can be used for healing, relaxation, and many other purposes. Oils can be diluted and used as an ointment, you can disperse the aromas with an essential oil burner, or you can place a few drops in your bathtub. These oils are simple to use, effective, and smell great!

Chapter 7:

More Tools to Ease Stress

In this chapter, we will look at more tools you can use to ease stress, especially in times of shadow work. We'll be looking at how you can ground yourself and improve stability, how you can use the emotional freedom technique and the benefits of massage therapy. Perhaps one of the most powerful ways to experience nature is by bathing in her beauty.

Healing Through Nature

By grounding yourself you connect with the Earth and can then benefit from this connection's healing properties. If you are a sensitive, you probably feel drawn to nature. You are more aware of its beauty and revitalizing quality, as spending time in a place such as a forest can help in calming your mind and body, and promote healing.

Sensitives are drawn to nature, such as forests and parks, as these beautiful and tranquil places help ground us and give us our much-needed peace. The Japanese created a term for spending time in the forest for the purpose of healing and finding tranquility—*shinrin-yoku*, which means "taking in the forest atmosphere," or simply put, "forest bathing." Forest bathing helps us as sensitives to process, manage, and discard emotional baggage.

Nature and Her Desire to Help Us

You are certainly already aware that spending time in nature is beneficial. If you have never truly spent time among the trees, now is a good time to start. You'll have a chance to escape from the demands and pressure of your daily life. You will have to search far and wide to find a more peaceful place than nature. Just walking alongside trees can restore tranquility in your heart. Spending just five minutes between trees or in other green spaces can boost your physical and mental well-being. I found this so wonderful and inspiring that I became a guide myself. I've learned about forest bathing techniques and nature connectedness skills to promote mindfulness in nature. Some benefits of spending time in forests and among trees are:

- improving your mood
- an increase in positive energy levels
- combat high blood pressure
- acceleration of recovery after surgery or during an illness
- reduced levels of stress
- improving your quality of sleep
- boosting your immune system
- an increase in the ability to concentrate

Plants and trees produce chemicals called *phytoncides* which help the plants fight off insects and bad bacteria. It also has antifungal properties. These compounds become airborne, which means we breathe it in while we spend time in the forest. This activates our bodies to produce white blood cells called natural killer (NK) cells. This type of white blood cell attacks and kills virus-infected and tumorous cells if they are present in our bodies. Miraculous, isn't it? Nature is gentle and tranquil, yet works hard to heal us.

Just looking at trees while spending time among them improves your mood, reduces stress, and lowers your blood pressure. As stress negatively impacts your immune system, looking at trees will not only reduce anger, fatigue, depression, confusion, and anxiety but will also improve your body's ability to heal. If you happen to live in an urban area, don't worry. Just look around your neighborhood. You should find a green space somewhere close by, such as a park. Perhaps it won't be as impactful as strolling in the forest, but it will still bring about a big positive change to your health.

It may be that you have to juggle a hundred tasks a day with a multitude of things demanding your attention and focus—your job, kids, partner, car, house, and more. Being in the forest and observing the birds, plants, water, and just the overall beauty of nature will give the cognitive part of your brain a much-needed break, which will recharge you mentally and restore your focus.

Benefits of Forest Bathing

As a child, I felt a deep and strong connection with nature. I even felt a bond with some of the trees near my home, in some way considering them to be my *friends*. Did you have a similar experience? In all the work and research that I have done, I found that this is not uncommon among sensitives. Many of us feel the same way. Of course, this caused the other kids to think of me as a *weirdo*. As they say, boys will be boys, but whenever some boys were needlessly breaking branches of a tree or damaging its bark, I would fight them off (although sensitives are rarely fighters).

For some time I thought I was the only *weird* kid until I met Larry. He felt the same way I did, and I have to admit that I was somewhat surprised to learn that Larry even had names for some of the trees. I'm not talking about pine or apple trees. No, he actually named the trees as parents would name their children. One day, as we were walking among the trees, he said that *Davon* was in pain. This puzzled me. We walked until we reached a certain tree. A quick search and Larry found and removed a nail.

Someone had hammered this nail into a tree, and Larry sensed it!

Did you know that you too can sense a tree's vibrational energy? To experience it, stand with your back against a tree and touch it with the palms of your hands. Relax and feel whether the energy flows upward or downward. According to Dr. Maja Kooistra, author and research scientist at the Ministry of Agriculture, Nature Management, and Fisheries in the Netherlands, trees can be divided into two groups, namely solar and lunar trees. *Solar trees* direct their energy into the ground, while *lunar trees* direct their energy upward. You probably already know how to tell the difference innately: Solar trees (oak, ash, walnut, pine) bloom in more wide and wild patterns, reaching their branches up towards the sun, while lunar trees (willow, beech, spruce, chestnut) store their energy in their roots, grow low and deep into the ground, and often have a harder bark shell or canopy to protect the trunk from direct sunlight.

If you would like your mind to be cleared, I invite you to stand with your back against a lunar tree for a while. If you feel the need to be grounded, find a solar tree and feel the energy flowing toward the Earth.

To engage in the practice of forest bathing, go into a forest where it is calm, yet still safe. Observe everything around you. What do you see? What colors can you distinguish? What sounds do you hear? Do you hear animals and birds, or perhaps the bubbling of a stream? Observe the pace of your steps. What does it sound like as you walk around? What do you smell? What does the ground smell like? How about the trees and plants? What do you feel? Do you feel a cool breeze and sunlight on your face? While you are forest bathing, don't think too much about your environment. The objective is to let your senses do all the work.

Immerse yourself in the beauty of nature and let the forest do its work.

There are retreats focused on forest bathing, helping people connect with nature for healing and relaxation. One of these institutions (which is also my personal favorite) is The Mindful Tourist (TMT). You can enjoy some time in the forest, or if you are interested, be trained to become a forest bathing guide. Is it worth it? For sure! I should know because I did it. There is a lot to learn, but it is learning with no stress or negative emotion. Everything you learn is insightful, beautiful, and inspiring.

Emotional Freedom Technique

Sensitives are called *sensitives* for a good reason: We are sensitive to everything and everyone. Our emotions can run wild and often get mixed with the emotions of others. We don't only live our own experiences, but often also the experiences of others. *Emotional freedom technique,* or *EFT tapping,* is the perfect way to deal with this. It is an alternative method for treating emotional distress and physical pain. It is also known as psychological acupressure. This method involves tapping the body to restore the balance of energy, reduce pain, and deal with difficult emotions.

Although around 20% of people are sensitive, it can be hard to find another sensitive who truly understands you. Larry was the first other sensitive I ever met, for which I am grateful, as we understand each other, at least most of the time. Many non-sensitives such as family members, friends, and colleagues don't understand or appreciate what it means to be a sensitive. They will often say things like, "*Why are you upset? I don't understand why you are acting this way, Can't you just get over it?* or *It really wasn't that bad."* Do some of these phrases sound familiar?

It is frustrating to see other people, including those who belittle your sensitivity, seem so lighthearted, happy, and confident all the time. It makes us as sensitives wonder if these people ever have to deal with emotional baggage. Mostly, it doesn't seem that way. Sensitives can be angered or become agitated easily sometimes. It's not our fault. However, please don't think I'm giving all sensitives the green light for behaving rudely. Besides, sensitives are kind, caring, and considerate people.

How to Practice EFT Tapping

I'll be honest, the first time I encountered EFT tapping, it seemed a little bit strange to me. But after I have tried it, I found it to be unconventional but highly effective. It is a method used by many therapists worldwide. It involves tapping on parts of the body with two or four fingers while saying phrases that acknowledge your emotions. The tapping of the body or parts of the face affects the nervous system and causes the production of cortisol and adrenaline, the stress hormones, to shut down. Let's look at how you can do EFT tapping—oh, remember, please do this only when it is safe to do so. For example, don't try it while driving.

While some jump to dismiss this theory as pseudoscience, it's really no different than mindful meditation with a purpose, as the physical touch grounds you to the present (which is hopefully a safe space) while you allow your mind to work through difficult feelings, phobias, or memories. The specific places to tap correlate to acupuncture points, so make sure you see a professional if you're serious about learning more about this technique. It's also important to have someone with experience leading EFT to make sure you are not overwhelmed by what may come up, be it eye-opening, relieving, or unpleasant.

When you are tapping your hand, you will be tapping the side of your hand where your pinky is, just below the pinky to your wrist, using the tips of your pointer, middle, and ring finger, and the pinky of your other hand. For example, if you are tapping your right hand, you will use the four fingertips of your left hand. When you are tapping parts of your face or your collar bones, you'll be using the tips of your pointer and middle fingers. You can use either one or both hands for tapping the parts of your face and collarbones. There are many more places and patterns to learn and try; if you like energy medicine, this could prove useful and powerful.

If you'd like to include EFT tapping as part of shadow work, I suggest you visit *www.highsensitives.com* and look for their section on EFT tapping for highly sensitive people, or you can visit *www.emofree.com*.

Finding Release Through Massage Therapy

Sensitives are primarily "givers" rather than "takers." We love to spoil other people and treat them with gifts and kind gestures, but often struggle to receive favors in return. But, we *should* also be treated kindly and gently and we owe it to ourselves to do so.

Massage therapy can greatly improve your shadow work experience.

How Massage Therapy Improves Shadow Work

Massage therapy is focused on connecting your emotional history and trauma with the physical manifestations within your body. It helps you to connect your muscles and autonomic nervous system to your emotional experience. Basically, you are uploading a mental experience into your physical body, so it can be removed through massage therapy. You can find release from trapped trauma and tension, and have a chance to reconnect with your body. If you haven't tried massage therapy, I strongly recommend it. These therapists are professionally trained to help you heal physically and mentally.

As a sensitive, it is often difficult to respond to situations or people without them thinking that you may be losing your mind. Massage therapy can help improve your emotional responses, how you handle emotions during an emotional event, the overall well-being of your body, and how your body reacts to emotional situations. As children, sensitives often create coping mechanisms as we try to survive the onslaught of life. These mechanisms aren't left in our childhood. It is brought with us into our adult life. If the mechanisms aren't dealt with, they will continue to affect the way we think and behave.

The therapists prefer to create a type of relationship between themselves and their clients. A massage therapist will ensure that their client becomes fully aware of how their body is feeling, namely in their skin, muscles, connective tissues, and joints. Through this process, the therapist will be able to determine the exact spot where the tension resides. The therapist will often be able to tell the client where the tension originated, such as an emotional situation. Then, the therapist helps the client to get rid of the tension (and the possibility of future tension in the same area) by helping the client deal with the emotional situation that caused the tension.

Massage therapy can also help with grief, depression, stress, and anxiety. The therapist does this by bringing the client's body back to feeling the way it should, which is calm, relaxed, and balanced. This, in turn, will help the client to feel safe and happy. Massage therapy is perfect to use during shadow work, as shadow work focuses on what is happening in your head, while massage therapy is focused on what is happening in your body.

Hi, I'm Your Shadow; Nice to Meet You

Get ready to say "hello" to your little friend; in this section, we'll be looking at the importance of grounding when practicing shadow work.

Grounding Yourself—An Essential Embodiment Practice

As shadow work can be a painful process, especially for sensitives, it is important to do grounding before attempting shadow work. *Grounding* is exactly what it sounds like—it connects you to the Earth, your environment, and yourself. It serves as a steadfast foundation that will help you to stand while you are bombarded with a flood of intense and difficult emotions. These emotions can include jealousy, anger, or greed. Shadow work can cause you to feel like you are losing control, which makes grounding the anchor that will help you hold on to reality.

As sensitives, many of us have developed the skill of "leaving our bodies." We can allow our minds to travel anywhere, as long as our consciousness is not in the present moment. This happens when we are in an emotional or traumatic situation. However, for shadow work to be successful, you need to be in your body in the present moment. Shadow work breaks you down to your core until it is revealed who you truly are. You may question your identity, even becoming unsure of who you are supposed to be. While your mind may be going in many directions, your body remains in one place. Grounding makes your body the place you can come back to whenever you need to.

During shadow work, your body is like a ship that you take right into a fierce storm. While the storm is frightening and feels threatening, you trust in the safety of your ship. Through grounding, you have ensured that your anchor is tight and secure, which means that you cannot drift away meaninglessly. Your mind will be traveling in various directions: into the past, alternate realities as you think about how things could have been different, and into the future as you think about how things could be. This is why your body must be anchored.

Sensitives view the Earth as a protective mother. Grounding creates a direct connection with the Earth. When you establish this connection, you share the Earth's energy and make it your own. This will make shadow work more significant—the journeys you go through to find healing and peace will not only be for yourself but the planet as well. The Earth *wants* to provide you with nurture, safety, and wisdom. It is available to you. Just reach out and take it. Then use it.

Grounded Meditation for Shadow Work

For focus and clarity, you need to ground yourself before starting your meditative session. You connect with the energy of your physical environment and the spiritual energy around you. Let's look at some methods you can use to establish your connection with the earth.

- Walking barefoot on grass is a great way to allow the Earth's energy to connect with your own. You can also walk on wet sand or dirt. While you are walking, focus on how the Earth feels beneath your feet. Allow your energy to connect with the energy of the Earth.
- Make a different connection by interacting with a tree or another living organism.
- You can also use earthing patches, earthing bands, or an earthing mat to strengthen your connection to the Earth's energy while you meditate.

Why Grounding Is So Powerful

Many sensitives use their time in nature for a practice called *grounding* or *earthing*. During this practice, you are in nature, standing on the ground barefoot. Image roots growing from underneath your feet deep into the earth. There's a science to it—the Earth contains vast amounts of electrons. Because of modern-day living, we do not come in touch with the electrons anymore. These electrons can enter our bodies while we practice grounding. They have healing properties and are powerful in healing us mentally and physically. Some people can't get to forests or green areas, unfortunately. But that doesn't mean that there's no hope. You can buy an earthing sheet or any other earthing product that you find available. You can use this sheet, or product, while you are sleeping. The product, such as an earthing sheet, connects you to the Earth and provides you with healing electrons.

Grounding is all about making contact with the Earth. Besides, walking barefoot is healthier than wearing shoes—unless you're walking over urban streets with broken glass or scalding hot concrete. Most nerve endings are found in the soles of our feet.

This enables us to establish deeper connections with the Earth. I believe that this is the reason our feet sometimes sweat. The moisture allows our feet to become more conductive, thereby allowing a stronger connection to the Earth. Let's take a look at some evidence-based benefits of grounding:

- improved the quality of sleep
- a decrease in pain
- a decrease in stress response
- quicker healing of wounds
- healed inflammation
- improved cortisol rhythm
- reduced blood viscosity
- increased heart rate variability which improves emotional resilience, recovery, and overall well-being (Missimer, 2021)

The Big Finale

In this section, with your knowledge and tools in place, you'll find some suggested steps into the dark and adventurous practice of shadow work.

Dedicate Time and Space

Shadow work can take a long time. If you are planning to do shadow work, make sure that you have enough time to be alone—which excludes, of course, a person you want to be with you for support. If someone is with you, don't make funny comments or jokes about shadow work. It is quite serious and honestly no laughing matter. Your mental and physical health depends on the success of your session of shadow work. You can listen to guided meditations for shadow work, which is why a guided meditation is included in this book. You can also find other guided meditations that are suitable for sensitives to help guide you through your process of shadow work.

Make sure your space is as comfortable as possible, with enough blankets, pillows, and drinks, such as water or tea. You can light some candles for ambiance and incense for aroma. Sit down comfortably for some time, deeply thinking about yourself. Ask yourself which of your aspects you dislike and feel is worthy of rejection. If you need help, you can listen to the guided meditation.

Shining a Spotlight on Your Shadow

Be fully aware of how you feel and keep track of your emotions. You can identify your shadow through emotional responses. You'll know you have touched on your shadow when you feel fear, disgust, sadness, irritation, anger, or any other negative emotion. Your body will react to your shadow as well, through things such as becoming uncomfortable, feeling chills, shaking, and increased heat. Talk to your shadow. Tell your shadow that you are not angry, but forgiving. Let your shadow come into the light gently and carefully.

Start Writing

Write down everything about yourself that you don't like. Also write down things in others that you don't like (disliking something in another person often mirrors something we don't like about ourselves, subconsciously). Carl Jung stated, "Everything that irritates us about others can lead us to an understanding of ourselves" (Mr Purrington, 2019). This type of writing is non-confrontational, but rooted in the need for self-love, which means it is a perfect method for sensitives. Keep in mind that the entire process of shadow work should not be rushed. It can take many hours, so be patient. After you have written all your dislikes, write down everything you like about yourself and others. Next, write down all the beliefs you have that you think are damaging and then all the beliefs you have you believe are positive and good for your overall well-being. Write every new thing on a new line.

Understand that there is a law that is applicable here. It is called the *law of duality*. All people have a shadow self. Some of the things you love seeing in others are part of your shadow, while some of your best traits are part of other people's shadows. And all of this is perfectly natural. It is like *yin and yang*, all of mankind has a light and shadow self.

Categorize and Rate

Next, try to categorize all of the things you don't like, such as love, body, and emotions. Don't worry about how many categories there should be. It is completely up to you. Next, determine how strong their presence is in your life. Give them a rating between one and ten.

Accept That Your Shadow Is a Part of You

Look at everything you have written. This is who you are. You may feel flawed, but remember, this is how we *all* were created. Humankind is flawed. This keeps us humble and grateful. Those who don't want to accept their flaws are doomed to self-loathing and self-resentment. If we can accept who we are, we can live in peace and harmony with our shadow selves.

Decide That You Will Love Your Shadow

Your shadow is not a separate part of you. It is part of who you are. There is no changing that. Just as you accept and love all that is good about you, you should do the same for your shadow. Your experiences and pain brought your shadow to life. When you have unconditional love for your shadow, you will have a love for yourself and those around you. Look upon your shadow with kindness and mercy, like a loving parent would look at their imperfect child.

Keep in mind that you may have to do shadow work several times before you find the healing you desire. Making peace with another person doesn't just fix things instantly. It is the same with your shadow. Living with your shadow is an adjustment that can be challenging at times.

Understand the Role of Your Shadow

When you have identified your shadow, you can now live in acceptance. Remember that there is a difference between identifying your shadow and identifying *with* your shadow. Although your shadow is part of who you are, you are *not* your shadow. Some aspects of your shadow cannot change, but you can still manage these traits and stop reacting whenever they are triggered.

Living With All That You Are

As you adjust and accept that you must live with all your aspects, both light and shadow, you become stronger, wiser, and empowered. There is inexplicable freedom that comes with accepting one's shadow. You'll be braver, more authentic, and more compassionate. You'll even be able to love and accept others when they show you their dark side.

Above all, understand that one of the most important traits you can have is acceptance. And accepting yourself is far more important than gaining or craving the acceptance of others. I place into my words all my love and energy so you can make it your own. You are a worthy person. You are sensitive but strong, kind but fierce, vulnerable yet powerful.

Conclusion

As a sensitive, it is essential to do shadow work. The world can be overwhelming and taxing, draining us of positive energy, or injecting us with negative energy. We need to find balance, healing, and tranquility to which there is a powerful solution—shadow work.

Being sensitive is an innate trait shared by sensitives and empaths and is associated with higher responsivity to environmental and social stimuli. In simpler words, a sensitive's brain reacts with a heightened response when it comes to memory, self-other processing, and awareness. However, we are not simply biochemical machines where who we are is determined by our DNA. We have the ability to create and unfold our own lives. This means we are not the victims of genetics or circumstance but have the power to take control of our lives and live the way we want to.

Did you know that your genes turn on and off, depending on your circumstance or environment? Where you live, who you interact with, and what you eat will influence the expression of your genes. Your genes are a blueprint, which means they will activate according to your environment and the perception of those you closely interact with. Sensitives need nourishing environments and have the potential of becoming change-makers, leaders, environmental activists, or someone who can express their creativity, such as writers and painters.

In Chapter 1, we learned about people who are sensitive. We saw that they can be divided into three groups: sensitives, highly sensitive people, and empaths. Sensitives and highly sensitive people are more attuned to their environment and other people.

They experience emotions and sensory input on a much deeper level. Empaths can be emotional sponges, absorbing the emotions of others. This can cause confusion as the empath can't always distinguish between their own emotions and that of others. It is important to remember that being a sensitive is not a disability or a burden, but a gift. If you are a sensitive, learn to love and embrace this and understand that there is a purpose for your gift.

In Chapter 2, we talked about the importance of improving your self-esteem before starting with shadow work, as shadow work can be challenging. Facing aspects that are suppressed into your shadow self can cause negative emotions, fear, and anxiety. For this reason, it is a good idea to incorporate meditation into your shadow work session. Meditation clears your mind and has a calming effect. For shadow work to be successful, you need to be as calm and level-headed as possible. There are several aspects that feel uncomfortable that will come into the light, such as false beliefs, fears, and trauma. You were then provided with a guided meditation that helps with shadow work. It guides you to bring your shadow self into the light, embrace and accept it, and make the decision to accept yourself fully for all you are.

In Chapter 3, we examined energy and how it affects us. Sensitives tend to draw energy from other people and their environments, whether these energies are positive or negative. Sensitives need to shield themselves from negative energy. Words that are thought, read, or spoken contain energy that can be transferred. Sensitives can easily pick up on the energy of others and pick up on their intention, simply by observing their body language, facial expressions, words, and vibrations. Because sensitives are easily overwhelmed by sensory information, they are more vulnerable to illness. Stress and anxiety caused by sensitivity can be harmful to the sensitive's immune system, impairing their bodies' ability to protect them from becoming ill. This makes shadow work even more essential.

In Chapter 4, we discussed the power of the mind. We are being *programmed* from a very young age. The things we are taught program our minds, such as beliefs of the family, culture, and close society and what the people around us view as acceptable and unacceptable. Our brains consist of three parts, the cerebellum, the cerebrum, and the brain stem. The cerebellum is the conscious mind and the part we use for purposes such as conscious decision-making, judgment, and learning. The cerebrum is a smaller part of the brain and is where the subconscious resides. Many of the things that we suppressed can be found here. The information stored in the cerebrum is what triggers us when we see something that causes an emotional response. We then talked about mindsets, and how you can go about reprogramming your mind.

In Chapter 5, we looked at tools you can use to heal your body, mind, and spirit. Tools for healing your body include taking a mindful bath, using hand gestures called *mudras*, exercising, smiling, and using crystals. Tools for healing your mind include breathing exercises, cutting connections with relationships that no longer serve a purpose, and smoke cleansing. Tools for healing your spirit include purifying your aura, meditation, practicing gratitude, and using the sounds of bells, chimes, and water.

In Chapter 6, we talked about how you can use sound and smell as tools for healing. Music is powerful and can easily change a person's mood. Relaxing music can improve your body's immune system, calm you down, and help you to get a good night's sleep. Dancing is a very effective way to clear your body from negative energy. We read the story about Petra Biro, a professional ballet dancer who discovered the benefits of dancing at a young age. As a sensitive, Petra was struggling with emotions and stability, until she started dancing. We then turned to smells and discussed the benefits of several essential oils that are perfect for sensitives and shadow work.

In Chapter 7, we examined the powerful effect nature has on sensitives. Trees and plants give off chemicals called phytoncides, which protect plants and trees from bacterial and fungal infections. As you walk through the forest during a session of forest bathing and breathe in this chemical, it activates your body to create natural killer white blood cells. These cells target cells that are tumorous and infected with viruses. Grounding is essential, as it provides stability during shadow work. The Earth contains countless electrons that have a positive healing effect on your body.

We learned that trees can be divided into two groups, according to their flow of energy. There are solar trees where the direction of their energy flow is toward the Earth, and lunar trees where the direction of their energy flow is upward, toward the sky. You can experience the energy flow by standing against the tree with your back and placing your palms on the tree. The energy from lunar trees can be used to clear your mind, while the energy from solar trees can be used for grounding yourself. We also discussed emotional freedom technique, or EFT tapping, and how to practice it. We then talked about the benefits of incorporating massage therapy into shadow work. Having the emotional baggage manifest in your body massage therapy is effective in removing the tension physically.

If you found this book to be inspiring to you or helpful in any way, please kindly leave a positive review on Amazon—with your own story if you're comfortable with it.

Now that you have all the tools you need and more, you can do shadow work safely, embracing and loving all that is a part of you.

You can't run from your shadow, but you can invite it to dance.

References

Aarding™. (n.d.). *A great revolution for our well-being? (Deepak Chopra)*. Aarding™. Retrieved May 9, 2022, from https://aarding.org/pages/earthing#

ABC News. (2006, January 6). *GMA: Auras gain recognition*. ABC News. https://abcnews.go.com/GMA/story?id=127539&page=1

Aipassa, M. (2021). *How to deal with weather sensitivity using this mudra*. Balance Your Energy. https://balanceyourenergybyvitaltouch.com/how-to-deal-with-weather-sensitivity-using-this-mudra/

Alcantara, M. (2016, April 12). *Alcantara acupuncture & healing arts» Why smudging your body with white sage is a must for every highly sensitive warrior (a guide to smudging)*. Alcantara. https://alcantaraacupuncture.com/why-smudging-your-body-with-white-sage-is-a-must-for-every-highly-sensitive-warrior/

Alchemy with Mirrah. (2020). *Why do we hide our true self? - Brené Brown on shame & vulnerability TED talk speaker* [YouTube Video]. In YouTube. https://www.youtube.com/watch?v=uFAwbcPa8l4

Anthony, K. (2018, September 18). *EFT tapping*. Healthline. https://www.healthline.com/health/eft-tapping#:~:text=Emotional%20freedom%20technique%20(EFT)%20is

Aron, E. N. (2019, November 12). *Meditation for highly sensitive people*. Psychology Today. https://www.psychologytoday.com/us/blog/the-highly-sensitive-person/201911/meditation-highly-sensitive-people

Barton, N. (2022, January 5). *Essential oils for shadow fears & manifesting abundance*. Base Formula. https://www.baseformula.com/blog/shadow-fears-abundance

Bauder, P. (2021, June 11). *How to survive and thrive as a highly sensitive person, with Bevin Niemann of Perceptive Souls*. Authority Magazine. https://medium.com/authority-magazine/how-to-survive-and-thrive-as-a-highly-sensitive-person-with-bevin-niemann-of-perceptive-souls-ced0f0d2f184

Biro, P. (2020, April 29). *Dance and yoga for HSPs: A professional ballet dancer's story*. Highly Sensitive Society. https://www.highlysensitivesociety.com/blog/dance-and-yoga-for-hsps-a-professional-ballet-dancers-story

Bjelland, J. (2020, June 27). *Tools to make life easier as a highly sensitive person with Julie Bjelland*. Julie Bjelland. https://www.juliebjelland.com/hsp-blog/tools-to-make-life-easier-as-a-highly-sensitive-person-with-julie-bjelland

Brackett, M. (2019, November 26). *How your negative emotions can literally make you sick*. Medium; Elemental. https://elemental.medium.com/how-your-negative-emotions-can-literally-make-you-sick-e6d8f363432a

Breuer-Udo, A. (2020, April 22). *The real truth about meditation for HSP's*. Annabelle Breuer-Udo. https://www.evocativehealthpath.com/meditation-for-highly-sensitive-people/

Burgin, T. (2022, January 30). *24 ways to clear negative energy from your body and home*. Yoga Basics.

https://www.yogabasics.com/connect/yoga-blog/clear-negative-energy/

Chevalier, G., Sinatra, S. T., Oschman, J. L., Sokal, K., & Sokal, P. (2012). *Earthing: Health implications of reconnecting the human body to the Earth's surface electrons.* Journal of Environmental and Public Health, 2012, 1–8. https://doi.org/10.1155/2012/291541

Cho, A. (2021, January 26). *The basic principles of feng shui.* The Spruce. https://www.thespruce.com/what-is-feng-shui-1275060

Cleveland Clinic. (2021, June 21). *Brainstem: Overview, function & anatomy.* Cleveland Clinic. https://my.clevelandclinic.org/health/body/21598-brainstem#:~:text=Your%20brainstem%20is%20the%20bottom

Coholic, D. (2005). *The helpfulness of spiritually influenced group work in developing self-awareness and self-esteem: A preliminary investigation.* The Scientific World Journal, 5, 789–802. https://doi.org/10.1100/tsw.2005.99

Collins, D. (2021, August 17). *Can listening to music reduce stress? Research, benefits, and genres.* Psych Central. https://psychcentral.com/stress/the-power-of-music-to-reduce-stress

Cooks-Campbell, A. (2021, August 19). *Breathwork: The secret to emotional regulation.* BetterUp. https://www.betterup.com/blog/breathwork

Cotec, I. (2021, December 1). *Shadow work guided meditation: Integrating your shadow - HeroRise.* HeroRise.

https://www.herorise.us/shadow-work-guided-meditation/

CricketSong. (2010). *What is an empath?* YouTube. https://www.youtube.com/watch?v=8NJciKB-uLU

De Vitto, J. (2021, January 4). *Why the highly sensitive person is more than genetics.* Highlysensitivehumans. https://www.highlysensitivehumans.com/post/why-the-highly-sensitive-person-is-more-than-genetics

Department of Environmental Conservation. (2012). *Immerse yourself in a forest for better health.* New York State. https://www.dec.ny.gov/lands/90720.html

Eby, D. (2022, March 27). *Rue Hass on using EFT to help highly sensitive people.* Highly Sensitive. https://highlysensitive.org/77/counselor-rue-hass-on-using-eft-to-help-highly-sensitive-people-celebrate-their-positive-qualities/

Eileenburns. (2018, June 17). *Essential oils for empaths and highly sensitive people.* Eileen Burns. https://eileenburns.co.uk/essential-oils-for-empaths/

Eisler, M. (2017, April 28). *5 Healing benefits of listening to music.* Chopra. https://chopra.com/articles/5-healing-benefits-of-listening-to-music

Elliott, C. H., & Smith, L. L. (2006). *Anxiety & depression workbook for dummies.* Wiley.

Fasano, R. (2020, September 24). *Releasing trapped emotions.* Spirituality & Health. https://www.spiritualityhealth.com/articles/2020/09/24/releasing-trapped-emotions

FightMediocrity. (2019, August 28). *Dr. Joe Dispenza - Learn how to reprogram your mind.* YouTube.

https://www.youtube.com/watch?v=rXGDAq6FnXo&t=36s

Ford, D. J. (2011, July 20). *How the brain learns.* Training Industry. https://trainingindustry.com/articles/content-development/how-the-brain-learns/

Frank, A. (n.d.). *Using EFT tapping for effective shadow work.* EFT Universe. Retrieved May 9, 2022, from https://eftuniverse.com/refinements-to-eft/using-eft-tapping-for-effective-shadow-work/

Giovanni. (2017, December 13). *Meeting your shadow self through meditation.* Live & Dare. https://liveanddare.com/your-shadow-self-and-meditation

Glad.is Admin. (2020, January 22). *Molecular biologist Bruce Lipton and the science behind good vibration.* Glad.is. https://glad.is/blogs/articles/molecular-biologist-bruce-lipton-and-the-science-behind-good-vibrations

Golden, J. (2020, January 29). *7 simple tools to clear negative energy from your space.* Mbglifestyle; mindbodygreen. https://www.mindbodygreen.com/0-17791/7-simple-tools-to-clear-negative-energy-from-your-space.html

Guziak, M. A. (n.d.). *Forest bathing certification training program.* The Mindful Tourist. Retrieved May 9, 2022, from https://themindfultourist.net/

Hass, R. (n.d.). *Healing with EFT tapping for the highly sensitive person.* EFT Universe. Retrieved May 9, 2022, from https://eftuniverse.com/hst/healing-with-eft-tapping-for-the-highly-sensitive-person/

Hass, R. A. (2009). *EFT for the highly sensitive temperament.* Energy Psychology Press.

Heid, M. (2018, April 26). *You asked: Is listening to music good for your health?* Time; Time.

https://time.com/5254381/listening-to-music-health-benefits/

Hill Riggs, J. (2019, January 28). *"Forest bathing" is a thing, and it can heal highly sensitive people*. Highly Sensitive Refuge. https://highlysensitiverefuge.com/forest-bathing-highly-sensitive-people/

Hill, M. (2019, October 23). *Your breathing matters*. Sensitive Evolution. https://sensitiveevolution.com/your-breathing-matters/

Hill, M. (2020, July 20). *Have you tried ecstatic dance?* Sensitive Evolution. https://sensitiveevolution.com/have-you-tried-ecstatic-dance/

Hrala, J. (2016, May 8). *Looking at trees can reduce your stress levels, even in the middle of a city*. ScienceAlert. https://www.sciencealert.com/urban-tree-coverage-can-significantly-reduce-stress-study-finds

HSP Point. (n.d.). *Breathing tips*. HSP Point. Retrieved May 9, 2022, from https://hsppoint.com/en/enextsubpage/7/36

Hughes, A. (2019, June 25). *The power of mudras*. Yogapedia. https://www.yogapedia.com/the-power-of-mudras/2/9117

Hunt, A. (2014, August 23). *Tapping into our shadow*. Practical Wellbeing. https://practicalwellbeing.co.uk/tapping-shadow/

Institute of Noetic Sciences. (2016). *Is mind over matter real? | Scientific Evidence* [YouTube Video]. In YouTube. https://www.youtube.com/watch?v=KukfeoZ7Y88

Isaacs, A. (2014). *Shadow work*. The Connection Coach. https://theconnectioncoach.co.uk/about-%26-contact

Jacobs Hendel, H. (2018, February 27). *Ignoring your emotions is bad for your health. Here's what to do about it*. Time; Time.

https://time.com/5163576/ignoring-your-emotions-bad-for-your-health/

Johnson, R. A. (2013). *Owning your own shadow: Understanding the dark side of the psyche.* Harper Collins.

Jung, C. G., Bly, R., Campbell, J., Hendrix, H., Scarf, M., Bradshaw, J., Hillman, J., Griffin, S., Wilber, K., Chernin, K., Peck, M. S., Sanford, J. A., Keen, S., May, R., Branden, N., Von Franz, M.-L., Downing, C., Dossey, L., Levinson, D. J., & Lorde, A. (1991). *Meeting the shadow: The hidden power of the dark side of human nature* (J. Abrams & C. Zweig, Eds.). Jeremy P Tarcher.

Kaushal, R. (2014, September 4). *Grounding is proven helpful for highly sensitive people.* HavingTime. https://havingtime.com/grounding-is-proven-helpful-for-highly-sensitive-people/

Kaushal, R. (2021, April 16). *The biggest mistake of sensitive people while practicing grounding.* Sensitive Evolution. https://sensitiveevolution.com/the-biggest-mistake-of-sensitive-people-while-practicing-grounding/

Kluge, G. (2020, February 2). *Mind over matter.* Theheartknows. http://www.theheartknows.org/mind-over-matter/

Kooistra, M. (2003). De kracht van bomen. Spirituele ontmoetingen tussen mens en natuur (Utrecht: Kosmos-Z&K/Servire).

Kooistra, M., "Unknown" @fredijhon. (2011, August 19). *Voice of the trees: Maja Kooistra.* Voiceofthetrees.blogspot.com. http://voiceofthetrees.blogspot.com/2011/08/maja-kooistra.html

Kurt. (2017, July 4). *Finding your centre: Grounding meditation techniques.* Earthing Canada.

https://earthingcanada.ca/blog/grounding-meditation-techniques/

Lawrence, G. (2021, December 16). *The science behind healing crystals explained | Dr David Hamilton*. YouTube. https://www.youtube.com/watch?v=8XVDFTOKiMo

Lee, K. A. (2021, March 3). *5 essential reasons to practice grounding before you start *any* shadow work*. The Moon School. http://www.themoonschool.org/shadow/5-reasons-grounding-before-shadow-work/

Liles, M. (2021, October 1). *Say "cheese!" 150 uplifting smile quotes that'll get you grinning from ear to ear*. Parade. https://parade.com/1045449/marynliles/smile-quotes/

Lipson, J. (n.d.). *Sensitives*. Spiral Wisdom LLC. Retrieved May 9, 2022, from https://www.spiralwisdom.com/counseling-guided-imagery/sensitives/

Luna, A. (2022, February 4). *Shadow work: The ultimate guide + free psychological test*. LonerWolf. https://lonerwolf.com/shadow-work-demons/

Malik, S. (2021, August 29). *10 mood-boosting essential oils for empaths & HSPs*. The Life Hype. https://thelifehype.com/essential-oils-for-empaths/

Malzer, C. (2019, October 1). *Music as medicine: How the power of music can help you heal*. The Conscious Club. https://theconsciousclub.com/articles/music-as-medicine-the-conscious-club

Malzer, C. (2020, July 30). *Move to heal: Here's how dancing improves happiness*. The Conscious Club.

https://theconsciousclub.com/articles/2019/10/9/move-to-heal-heres-how-dancing-improves-happiness

McCormick, K. (2021, September 6). *James receives Pilestone colorblind glasses for his 57th birthday.* YouTube. https://www.youtube.com/watch?v=sB-chLkLH3g

Melamed, M. (2021, May 26). *You should be dancing!* Age of Awareness. https://medium.com/age-of-awareness/you-should-be-dancing-18115f821d28

Merriam-Webster. (n.d.). *Mind over matter.* In Merriam-Webster.com Dictionary. https://www.merriam-webster.com/dictionary/mind%20over%20matter

Missimer, A. (2021, June 30). *The benefits of grounding | Earthing.* The Movement Paradigm. https://themovementparadigm.com/benefits-of-grounding/

Moberg, M. (2020, March 3). *Shadow work for sensitives.* Marci Moberg. https://www.marcimoberg.com/blog/2020/3/3/shadow-work-for-sensitives

Mr Purrington. (2019, December 14). *Carl Jung: "Everything that irritates us about others can lead us to an understanding of ourselves" in context.* Carl Jung Depth Psychology. https://carljungdepthpsychologysite.blog/2019/12/14/carl-jung-everything-that-irritates-us-about-others-can-lead-us-to-an-understanding-of-ourselves-in-context/#.Ynt_t-hBxqM

Myles, A. (2016, November 21). *Scientific facts that make me want to start smudging right now. | elephant journal.* Elephant Journal.

https://www.elephantjournal.com/2016/11/scientific-facts-that-make-me-want-to-start-smudging-right-now/

Nall, R. (2019, February 18). *Best essential oils for relieving anxiety.* Medical News Today. https://www.medicalnewstoday.com/articles/324478

Numerologist. (2019, December 2). *These 5 everyday herbs will make your deep dive into shadow work a ton easier (and more effective).* Numerologist. https://numerologist.com/health-and-well-being/herbs-shadow-work/

O, J. (2021, September 9). *10 mudras to reduce stress, anxiety and depression.* L'Aquila Active. https://laquilaactive.com/10-mudras-to-reduce-stress-anxiety-and-depression/

Orloff, J. (2019, January 11). *The difference between highly sensitive people and empaths.* Psychological and Educational Consulting. https://www.psychedconsult.com/the-difference-between-highly-sensitive-people-and-empaths/

Pandey, S. (2021). *How EFT tapping is a blessing for a highly sensitive person (HSP).* Tap Easy. https://tap-easy.com/eft-tapping-for-highly-sensitive-person/

Parato, S. (2020, April 20). *7 steps to release negative energy through dance - Purpose Fairy.* Purpose Fairy. https://www.purposefairy.com/82829/release-negative-energy-through-dance/

Pawula, S. (2021, July 5). *How to embrace your shadow & release your personal power.* Always Well Within. https://www.alwayswellwithin.com/blog/2014/07/06/embrace-your-shadow-side

Pou, J. V. (2011, November 2). *To see the light we must first acknowledge that we are in the dark.* Kokovoko. https://kokovoko.info/post/12255023720

Princing, M. (2021, September 1). *This is why deep breathing makes you feel so chill.* Right as Rain by UW Medicine;

RightAsRain. https://rightasrain.uwmedicine.org/mind/stress/why-deep-breathing-makes-you-feel-so-chill

Quinn, J. (2020, June 7). *How to do shadow work & reclaim your authenticity.* Consciousness Liberty. https://consciousnessliberty.com/how-to-do-shadow-work-reclaim-your-authenticity/

Raypole, C. (2019, November 24). *15 signs you might be an empath.* Healthline. https://www.healthline.com/health/what-is-an-empath

Redfearn, R. A. (2019). *Sensory processing sensitivity: Is being highly sensitive associated with stress and burnout in nursing?* [Thesis].

Rice, S. (2020, May 11). *5 grounding techniques for overstimulated HSPs.* Highly Sensitive Refuge. https://highlysensitiverefuge.com/5-grounding-techniques/

Riegler, T. (2020, June 2). *Am I really an empath or just sensitive HSP? Easy way to tell the difference!* YouTube. https://www.youtube.com/watch?v=ADmWgq_sJvU

Riegler, T. (2021, May 4). *Am I energy sensitive? Signs & tips to master your energy.* YouTube. https://www.youtube.com/watch?v=AZsZrF2GxSg

Rosieraleigh. (2019, August 1). *Why do we need to campaign for highly sensitive people?* Vantage. https://vantagesensitivity.org/2019/08/01/why-do-we-need-to-campaign-for-highly-sensitive-people/

ScarletScarlet. (2020, June 10). *Biological differences in nervous system of highly sensitive person.* Sintelly.

https://sintelly.com/articles/biological-differences-in-nervous-system-of-highly-sensitive-person

Shaw, J. (2020). *Evil: The science behind humanity's dark side*. Doubleday Canada.

Smit, A. W. (2017, April 12). *A simple and effective Japanese method to relax in 5 minutes-a lifesaver for HSP*. Anke Weber Smit. https://ankewebersmit.com/simple-effective-method-to-relax-5-minutes-hsp/

Sólo, A. (2020, March 30). *The difference between the highly sensitive brain and the "typical" brain*. Highly Sensitive Refuge. https://highlysensitiverefuge.com/highly-sensitive-person-brain/

Somatic Luminary. (2017, November 15). *The one essential oil every HSP needs*. Somatic Luminary. https://somaticluminary.com/the-one-essential-oil-every-hsp-needs/

Swan, T. (2015, April 5). *What is shadow work? - Teal Swan-*. YouTube. https://www.youtube.com/watch?v=2s8I3yq-Kmo

Terry, R. (2012, March 27). *Not glowing? 3 signs your energy is blocked*. Mbgmindfulness; mindbodygreen. https://www.mindbodygreen.com/0-4351/Not-Glowing-3-Signs-Your-Energy-Is-Blocked.html

The Connection Coach. (2020, July 24). *Shadow work and biodynamic massage - the perfect combination*. YouTube. https://www.youtube.com/watch?v=UhNxOgnkl9c

The Gary Craig Official EFTTM Training Centers. (2017). *What is official EFT?* Emofree.com. https://www.emofree.com/

Tribal Trade. (2020, May 21). *Benefits of smudging with sage (5 scientific reasons to smudge with sage!)*. Tribal Trade. https://us.tribaltradeco.com/blogs/smudging/benefits

-of-smudging-with-sage-5-scientific-reasons-to-smudge-with-sage

Tribal Trade Co. (2021, October 21). *How to smudge to reduce anxiety (achieve resilience by a smudging with sage)*. YouTube. https://www.youtube.com/watch?v=GRZqO_oU484

Walter, A.-K. (2021, August 16). *EFT tapping: A powerful personal growth tool for the highly sensitive person*. HiSensitives. https://hisensitives.com/blog/eft-tapping-highly-sensitive-person/

Wooll, M. (2021, December 20). *The benefits of shadow work and how to use it in your journey*. BetterUp. https://www.betterup.com/blog/shadow-work

Zweig, C., & Wolf, S. (1997). *Romancing the shadow: A guide to soul work for a vital, authentic life*. Ballantine Books.

Printed in Great Britain
by Amazon